FIRST STEPS IN THE KITCHEN

FIRST STEPS IN THE KITCHEN

Recipes for Young Beginners

by

MAUREEN O'CONNOR

illustrated by
Juliet Renny

FABER AND FABER
London

First published in 1971
by Faber and Faber Limited
3 Queen Square London WC1
Reprinted 1971
Printed in Great Britain by
Latimer Trend & Co Ltd Plymouth
All rights reserved

ISBN 0 571 09758 8 (Paper Covered Edition)
ISBN 0 571 09338 8 (Hard Bound Edition)

CONTENTS

CONTENTS

NOTE ON THE GRADING OF RECIPES

All the recipes in this book have been graded with a system of star symbols.

One star * means that this is a simple recipe for absolute beginners.

Two-star ** recipes are a little harder and should not be attempted until you have had plenty of practice with one-star recipes.

Three-star *** recipes are the hardest of all: most of the meat dishes have three stars and it is better not to attempt these until you have had plenty of practice in the kitchen using the easier recipes. When you are able to cook three-star dishes you should be ready to prepare a whole meal.

Chapter 1

ALL ABOUT THE COOKER

Before you start to cook have a look at the kitchen and all the things you are going to use. The best place to start is the cooker. Is your cooker electric or gas? Whichever it is it will have three main parts: a grill, several hotplates or burners, and an oven. With a gas cooker you can see the flames which are producing the heat, but with an electric cooker the heat may be almost invisible—but it will get just as hot.

ALL ABOUT A GAS COOKER

The gas comes to the cooker through a set of pipes and each pipe ends in a burner where the gas can be lit. There may be three or four small burners on the top of the cooker for boiling and frying on. There is a row of burners in the grill, and an even bigger row in the oven. Have a look at your cooker when everything is switched off, to make sure you know where all the gas burners are.

Lighting the gas

There are two ways of lighting a gas cooker.

Pilot lights

If your cooker is a modern one which has pilot lights, that is small gas burners which are always lit, it will light automatically when you turn the switch.

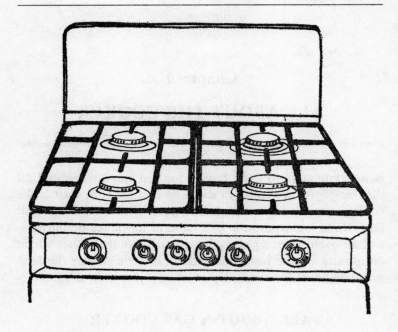

With a match

If your cooker has no pilot light, or if the oven or grill has no pilot light, you will have to use a match or a gas lighter to light the burners. The safest kind of gas lighter works from an electric battery.

Make sure first of all that you know which gas tap on the front of the cooker belongs to each burner. Usually they are labelled and the biggest tap, with a set of numbers round it, is the tap for the oven.

You may find that the oven has a small hole in the floor near the front. If so, you can light the oven by putting a flame in that hole instead of reaching right in to the burner at the back.

Safety first—how to light the gas

Follow these simple rules when you are lighting gas with a match or gas lighter.

1. Make sure you know which tap controls the burner you want.
2. Now take one match from the box.
3. Strike the match and hold it in your right hand (if you are right-handed).
4. Quickly turn on the gas tap with your other hand.
5. Hold the match about two inches from the burner which should then light.
6. If it does not light, turn off the gas tap quickly and blow out the match. Use a fresh match and start again.
7. You will always know when the gas is lit because you will be able to see, and probably to hear, the flames. NEVER leave a gas tap on unless you can see that the burner is safely lit.

How to control the gas

The amount of heat you get from the burners depends on the size of the flames. Turn the tap down low if you want to boil or grill something gently. Turn the flames up high if you want to fry or grill quite quickly. Do not boil things fiercely—there is no need.

The heat of the oven is controlled by the round dial on the tap, which is called the regulo. There are usually ten markings, from ½, which means a very cool oven, up to 9, which is very hot indeed. Once you have set the oven and it has had time to warm up, it will stay at the heat you have set it at until you alter the dial or switch it off.

ALL ABOUT AN ELECTRIC COOKER

An electric cooker usually has three or four hotplates for boiling and frying. These can either be of a solid black metal, or of a spiral of black metal which turns red when it is heated. The grill may be above or below the hotplates and this will also turn red as it is heated. The elements, that is the heated parts, of the oven are often invisible.

The different parts of the cooker are controlled by a row of switches at the front, one for each plate, one for the grill and a large one with figures round it for the oven. Make sure you know which switch belongs to each part of the cooker. This is especially important if you have the solid black hotplates because you will not be able to see whether they are on or off.

How to control an electric cooker

The hotplates and grills usually have switches with three different settings: high, medium and low. Or they may be numbered from 1 to 8 or 9, and in this case 1 will mean very low and 8 or 9 extremely hot. You will need a high setting for frying or bringing water to the boil quickly, and a medium setting for boiling more gently for a long period. A low setting will cook very slowly or just keep a pan warm.

The switch controlling an electric oven gives the various heats in degrees Fahrenheit, ranging from 200 which is very cool to 500 which is extremely hot. Turn the control knob to the heat you want and after it has warmed up the oven will stay at that heat until the switch is altered or turned off.

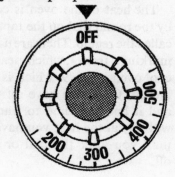

HOW TO USE YOUR COOKER

Once you are sure you know how your cooker works you can start thinking about using it, but remember that you are going to be dealing with very hot things—so take great care. Here are some hints which will help you to enjoy your cooking and avoid accidents.

The oven

1. Before you light the oven, make sure that the shelves are

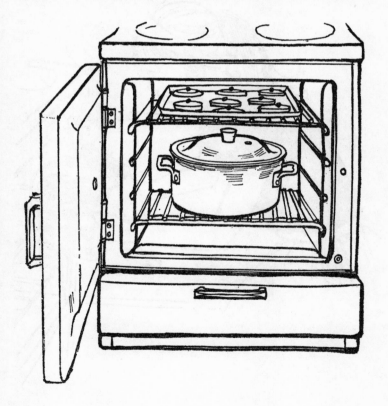

in the right place. Most ovens have at least two shelves which will slide out and can be put at different heights. Make your top shelf low enough to take the dish you are going to put on it. A pudding basin will need more room than a flat baking tray. Try to avoid moving the shelves once the oven is lit—they will be VERY HOT.

2. Always light or switch on your oven before you start preparing a recipe. This will give it time to warm up to the right heat before you put your dish in.

3. Heat rises upwards, so the hottest part of the oven will

always be the top shelf. Anything lower down will take a little longer to cook. The very bottom of the oven will be too cool to cook anything properly.

4. When things are cooking in the oven try not to open the door too often. The cooking times given in the recipes are about right so watch the clock carefully and take a peep about five minutes before the time is up just to make sure that everything is all right. Some dishes can be spoilt by a draught from the door.

5. When you have to move hot trays and dishes remember that *everything* in the oven will be very hot—the shelves, the sides of the oven and all the trays and dishes inside. Use a good thick oven cloth or gloves to protect your hands. NEVER use a cloth that is *wet* or *damp*. The heat will come straight through the wet material.

6. Before you take a hot dish out of the oven decide where you are going to put it. The best place is on top of the cooker or on a wire rack. NEVER put a pottery dish or basin which has come out of the oven straight on to a cold surface. It may break.

The top of the cooker

1. Make sure you know which switch controls the hotplate or grill you need.

2. Choose a hotplate which is the right size for the pan you want to use: some hotplates are smaller than others and they are the ones to use for small pans. A big pan will need a big hotplate.

3. Turn the heat to high to bring a pan to the boil, but once it is boiling turn the heat down and just keep the water boiling gently. So long as bubbles are coming to the surface the pan is still boiling, and there is no need to make clouds of steam or to have the pan so hot that it boils over or burns.

B

4. Do not fill pans too full: half-way or two-thirds up the side should be about right. If you need more liquid than that then use a larger pan.
5. Some things boil over more easily than others so keep an eye on all your pans. Milk is especially likely to boil over and should be watched *all the time*.

6. Grills get very hot, so watch food under them very carefully. *It can catch fire.*

7. Frying can be dangerous too if the pan gets too hot. Watch frying food *all the time.*

8. If you have to stir or mix anything in a pan on top of the cooker use a wooden spoon or a fish slice with a wooden or plastic handle. Metal handles can get too hot to hold.

9. Never leave spoons or forks in pans on the cooker. They can be knocked out, or even cause the pan to be knocked over.

10. Turn the handles of your pans *inwards* away from the edge of the cooker so that no one can knock against them and spill the pan. This is *very important.*

11. NEVER let small children near a cooker when it is being used.

Chapter 2

AROUND THE KITCHEN

Now here are some hints about the other tools you will need to use when you are cooking.

Mixing bowls

Most kitchens have a selection of bowls of different sizes for mixing things in. You will need a large bowl for making pastry, so that the flour does not spill over the top when you are rubbing it in, a medium-sized one for making a cake or pudding mixture, and a small bowl for beating up an egg.

Try to use a bowl which is the right size for the job, one that will hold all the ingredients and leave you enough room to stir them or beat them if necessary. And remember some things will increase in bulk as you beat them so you will need a fairly big bowl if you are going to whisk a lot of air into something like egg whites or cream.

Spoons

The best kind of spoon to use for mixing and stirring is a wooden one. These come in different sizes and are very cheap to buy. It is especially important to have a wooden spoon to stir anything hot as the handle will stay cool in a hot liquid.

Metal spoons come in different shapes and sizes: the ones used in cooking are usually teaspoons, dessertspoons and tablespoons and these are often used to give measurements, especially of liquids, in recipes.

Rolling pin and board

A rolling pin for rolling out dough can be of wood or pottery. If you do not have one, you can use a milk bottle turned on its side, but wash it very thoroughly first, and dry it on a clean cloth. The best thing for rolling pastry on is a thick wooden board, but any hard flat surface will do if you do not have a board. But again, make sure it is spotlessly clean before you put your dough on to it.

Pastry cutters

Pastry cutters come in different shapes and sizes and they make it easy to cut your rolled out pastry or dough into circles for tarts, scones or patties. If you do not have a pastry cutter find a glass or a cup which is about the same size as the edge of your patty pans, make sure it is quite clean and dry, and use the top of it to cut out your circles.

Patty pans and cake tins

These come in a number of different shapes and sizes. Patty pans are very useful for making pastry tarts and patties and for making small cakes. Large cakes are made in round or square tins. You may also find in the kitchen some even larger oven tins and dishes which are normally used for roasting meat. You will also need a flat metal baking tray for making biscuits and buns.

Whisks

There are several different kinds of whisk but they all serve the same purpose: to beat up food so that little bubbles of air go into the mixture. You may have a hand whisk with an end part of curved wire which beats the air into the mixture, or the kind where a handle turns metal blades which stir up the mixture very quickly. Or you may be able to use an electric

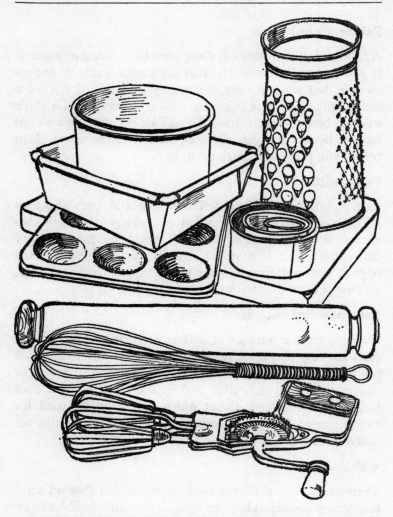

whisk which will do the job for you more quickly still. If you
do not have any sort of a whisk in the kitchen you can still
beat your mixture with a large fork, although this method
will be slower than with a proper whisk.

Graters

Graters may be different shapes but are usually made of metal
and have two or three sets of holes of different sizes. If you
rub food against the smallest holes it will be grated into fine
powder: these are used to grate things like nutmeg and very
hard cheese; the larger holes will shred vegetables or cheese
into strips of varying thickness. A grater is very useful when
making salads, for shredding up carrots, cheese, nuts, etc.

Knives and a chopping board

Most kitchens have a variety of knives but always remember
to use the right sort of knife for the job you want to do. For
cutting butter or trimming pastry a blunt table knife will do,
but if you want to peel or chop vegetables, and cut bread or
meat, you must have a really sharp knife to do the job. The
best knife for cutting bread is a long one with a serrated edge,
but for peeling vegetables a smooth straight-edged knife is
best, or you can use a potato peeler for things like carrots and

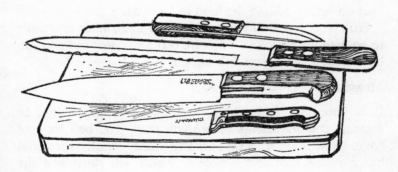

turnips. If you can, use a wooden chopping board when you
are cutting things so that you do not scratch the table top or
working surface.

Pans

Try to choose a pan which is the right size for the job. If you are only boiling a few vegetables take a small pan so that it is at least half full when your water and vegetables are together. But if you are making a big stew take a bigger pan which again will be about half full when everything is in. Never fill pans more than two-thirds full or they may boil over and make a mess or give you a nasty scald. Some things tend to swell and bubble when they are cooking. This can be controlled by turning down the heat or by removing the pan lid for a minute and then putting it on at an angle so that the steam can escape.

Frying pans and grills

Frying pans are sometimes made of heavy iron, so you will need two hands to lift these on to the stove. You can get frying pans which are specially treated so that the food will not stick to them, but with an ordinary frying pan food should not stick if you put your fat or oil in first and let it heat up before adding the food to be fried.

Grill pans are of different shapes and sizes, made especially to go with your cooker. The wire tray will come out and can be used as a rack to cool things on.

Measuring

It is important in cooking, and especially in baking, to measure the ingredients before you start. The best way, of course, is with scales. There are two kinds of scales. One kind has a round face and a pointer which will show you the weight of anything put into its pan. The other kind has two pans, one for the weights and one for the food you are weighing. There are usually six metal weights, from $\frac{1}{2}$ an ounce to 1 pound, and with combinations of these weights you can weigh up to 2 pounds of food. (Or if you have gramme weights you can weigh up to a kilo.) For instance, if you want to weigh 3 ounces of sugar, put the 2-ounce weight and the 1-ounce weight on to the small pan and fill the large pan with sugar until the two pans are exactly balanced.

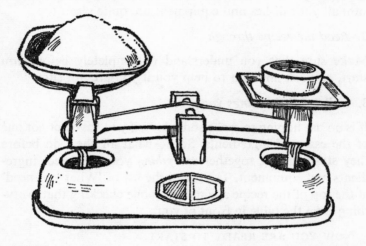

If you do not have scales there are some other simple ways of measuring.

FATS come in 8-ounce blocks, so

> 1 block = ½ pound
> ½ block = 4 ounces
> ¼ block = 2 ounces

FLOUR	1 heaped tablespoonful	= ⅔ ounce (20 grammes)
	1 level tablespoonful	= ⅓ ounce (10 grammes)
SUGAR	1 heaped tablespoonful	= 1 ounce (30 grammes)
	1 level tablespoonful	= ½ ounce (15 grammes)
EGGS	1 standard-sized egg	= 2 ounces (55 grammes)

To measure liquids use a measuring jug which will be marked in pints and fluid ounces.

Before you begin—three rules

1. *Wash your hands*

It is very important to keep food clean. Wash your hands and the table you are going to work on before you start. Make sure all your dishes and equipment are quite clean too.

2. *Read the recipe through*

Make sure that you understand it completely before you start, and ask an adult to help you if you are not sure.

3. *Collect all the things you need*

It is no use hoping to make something if you have not got one of the essential ingredients. So do what all chefs do before they start: collect together *everything* you will need, ingredients and equipment. Then read the list of 'What you need' at the top of the recipe again one by one checking that everything is on the table in front of you.

NOW YOU ARE READY TO START.

Chapter 3

ALL ABOUT BAKING

The first recipes in this book are for things mainly made with flour and baked in the oven: pastry for pies and tarts, cakes, scones and biscuits, most of them sweet but with a few savoury ones too.

Here are some hints which will help you every time you decide to bake.

Tins

Baking tins should always be greased and it is a good idea to make this your first task when you start work. First make sure that the tin is clean and dry, then grease the tin lightly but evenly all over with cooking oil or melted fat such as lard.

For some cakes greasing alone is not enough to stop the cake sticking to the tin. This is why some recipes advise you to sprinkle flour inside your greased tin, and for cakes which need a long time in the oven you will be told to line the tin with grease-proof paper. Do this by cutting a circle of paper for the bottom of the tin and a long strip for round the side.

If, in spite of your precautions, a cake should stick to the tin, do not worry. Use a broad-bladed knife or palette knife to ease the cake out of its tin and if it breaks stick the pieces together with a little jam. If you really want to hide a break in a cake, then you can always ice it.

Keep cool

When making pastry or scones it helps to keep yourself and your ingredients cool. If you are rubbing flour and fat together with your fingers hold your hands under the cold tap for a few minutes before you start, and then dry them. And if your hands warm up enough to make the fat melt and feel sticky, have a rest and cool your hands down again before you go on.

If you are one of those people who have naturally warm hands it may help to mix the fat and flour together with a fork instead of with your fingers.

It will also help if you keep the water or milk for pastry and scones in the refrigerator, or in a cool place, until you are ready to use it. And when the dough is finished do not handle it too much. Light fingers make much better pastry and scones.

Rolling out

Dough that is ready to roll out should never be too sticky, but you will find that it becomes more sticky as you roll it. Before you start, sprinkle flour on your board and on your rolling pin to stop the dough sticking. As you roll the dough thinner turn it over frequently and sprinkle more flour on the board underneath, on the pin and on top of the dough. This should prevent the dough sticking to the board or the pin while you are rolling.

When is it done?

The baking times given in the recipes will give you a good guide as to how long each dish will take to cook, but they cannot tell you exactly because every oven and dish will be slightly different. Pastry is done when it is crisp and a light golden brown colour. Scones are done when they have risen and are golden brown on top. Cakes are done when they are firm in the middle and regain their shape if they are pressed down with the back of a spoon or a knife blade.

Remember that it is not a good thing to open the oven door many times when anything is cooking. Cakes can be spoiled by a draught of cold air from the oven door. So be patient and wait until almost the time suggested in the recipe before you open the door to have a peep or to test to see whether a cake is done.

Chapter 4

HOW TO MAKE PASTRY

Short crust pastry *

What you need

8 ounces (225 grammes) self-raising flour
4 ounces (110 grammes) margarine OR 2 ounces (55 grammes)
    margarine and 2 ounces (55 grammes) white fat or lard
2 tablespoonfuls cold water
Mixing bowl
Knife
Teaspoon
Rolling board and rolling pin
A little extra flour for dusting the board

What to do

1. Put the flour into the mixing bowl.
2. Chop the fat into small pieces and put them into the bowl.
3. Use your fingertips, or a fork, to rub the mixture together
   very gently until it looks like fine bread crumbs.
4. Make a well in the middle of the mixture.
5. Add a little water and mix together with the blade of the
   knife until it makes a dough.
6. Add an extra tablespoon of water if the mixture will not
   stick together, but do not let it become sticky to touch.
7. Scatter some flour on your board and put the ball of dough
   in the centre.

8. Sprinkle more flour on top of the dough and on the rolling pin.
9. Roll out the dough until it is flat and about ⅛ inch (3 millimetres) thick.

Now your pastry is ready to cut into shapes to make into a number of different things.

Jam tarts *

What you need

Rolled out short crust pastry
Jam (or lemon curd or marmalade)
Teaspoon
Round pastry cutter about 2½ inches (6 centimetres) across
Patty tins about 2½ inches (6 centimetres) across

What to do

1. Cut the rolled out pastry into circles with the cutter.
2. Put one circle of pastry into each greased patty tin.
3. Press the circles down gently with your thumbs so that they fit the tins neatly.
4. Put a teaspoonful of jam into the centre of each tart. Do not fill them right up to the top or the jam will boil over in the oven.
5. Bake the tarts in a hot oven (Electric 400 °F., Gas 6) for 10 minutes.
6. Keep any left over pastry to make more tarts or something else.

Mince pies *

What you need

Rolled out short crust pastry
Jar of mincemeat

Teaspoon
Knife
Two round pastry cutters, one 2½ inches (6 centimetres) across, one 1½ inches (4 centimetres) across
Patty tins

What to do

1. Cut the rolled out pastry into the same number of large and small circles with the pastry cutters.
2. Put one large circle of pastry into each greased patty tin.
3. Press the pastry down gently so that it fits the tins neatly.
4. Put a teaspoonful of mincemeat in the centre of each pie.
5. Put a small circle of pastry on top of the mincemeat and press the edges of the two pastry circles together to close up the pie.
6. With the point of a knife make a small slit in the top of each pie.
7. Bake in a hot oven (Electric 400 °F., Gas 6) for 10 to 15 minutes until the pies are golden brown on top.

Sausage rolls *

What you need

Rolled out short crust pastry
8 ounces (225 grammes) sausage meat
Water
A little extra flour
Rolling board and pin
Knife
Flat baking tray

What to do

1. Roll the pastry into a long strip about 3 inches (8 centimetres) across.

2. With your fingers, make the sausage meat into a long thin sausage shape the same length as the strip of pastry. Dust it with flour if it is too sticky to hold.
3. Put the sausage meat into the centre of the strip of pastry and damp the edges of the pastry with water.
4. Roll the pastry strip right round the meat and press the edges together tightly.
5. Turn the long roll over so that the join is underneath.
6. Cut the roll into short lengths about 2 inches (5 centimetres) long.
7. Arrange the sausage rolls on the greased baking tray.
8. With the point of a knife cut two small slits in the top of each roll.
9. Bake in a hot oven (Electric 400 °F., Gas 6) for 20 to 25 minutes.

Apple pie **

What you need

Rolled out short crust pastry
1 pound cooking apples
2 tablespoonfuls sugar
Water
Pie dish or oven-proof plate
Sharp knife

What to do

1. Divide the pastry into two equal-sized pieces and roll out one piece until it is big enough to cover the bottom of the pie dish and about an eighth of an inch thick.
2. Fold this piece of pastry in half twice to make it easier to lift, and then unfold it on to the pie dish.
3. Press the pastry down to push out any air trapped underneath.

c

4. Trim the edge with a knife.
5. Peel the apples and cut the flesh in slices from the core.
6. Put the apple slices into the pastry-lined pie dish and sprinkle with the sugar.
7. Roll out the rest of the pastry to the right size for a lid for the pie dish.
8. Wet the edge of the lower piece of pastry with water.
9. Carefully lift the second pastry circle on to the dish on top of the apples and press the edges together firmly.
10. Trim the edge with a knife.
11. Decorate the edge of the pie with the knife handle or a spoon.
12. Cut two slits in the lid of the pie with the knife.
13. Bake in a hot oven (Electric 400 °F., Gas 6) for about 20 minutes.

Apple turnover * (A useful recipe to use up left-over pastry)

What you need

Short crust pastry
A cooking apple (or left-over stewed apples)
1 tablespoonful sugar
Water
Flat baking tray
Sharp knife

What to do

1. Roll out the pastry into a roughly circular shape.
2. Peel and slice the apple.
3. Place the apple slices (or the stewed apple) on one half of the circle of pastry, not letting it come too close to the edge, and sprinkle with the sugar.
4. Wet the edges of the pastry with water.

5. Turn the free half of the pastry circle over the apple and press the edges together firmly.
6. Turn the edge over to seal them and decorate them by pressing with a knife handle or spoon. This will also help to seal the edges tightly.
7. Make two small slits in the top of the turnover.
8. Place on the baking tray and bake in a hot oven (Electric 400 °F., Gas 6) for 20 minutes.

You can also make turnovers with jam instead of apple, or with some washed dried fruit sprinkled with a little brown sugar.

Cheese straws *

What you need

2 ounces (55 grammes) self-raising flour
2 ounces (55 grammes) margarine
3 ounces (85 grammes) grated Cheddar cheese
Pinch of salt and Cayenne pepper
1 egg yolk
2 tablespoonfuls water
Mixing bowl and wooden spoon
Rolling pin and board
Sharp knife
Flat baking tray
Cheese grater

What to do

1. Put the flour, salt and Cayenne pepper into the mixing bowl.
2. Chop the margarine into small pieces and add to the flour.
3. Rub the margarine into the flour with your fingertips until it looks like fine bread crumbs.
4. Grate the cheese and add it to the mixture.

5. Mix in the egg yolk with the wooden spoon and add enough water to make a stiff dough.
6. Roll out the dough to about ⅛ inch (3 millimetres) thick.
7. Cut into thin straw shapes, about 2 inches (5 centimetres) long and ¼ inch (6 millimetres) wide with a sharp knife.
8. Arrange the straws on the baking tray and bake in a hot oven (Electric 375 °F., Gas 5) for about 5 minutes, until golden brown and crisp.

Treacle tart *

What you need

Rolled out pastry
2 ounces (55 grammes) fresh bread crumbs
3 tablespoonfuls golden syrup
1 teaspoonful lemon juice
Pie dish or ovenproof plate
Knife
Mixing bowl and wooden spoon

What to do

1. Roll out the pastry into a circle large enough to fit the pie dish and about ⅛ inch (3 millimetres) thick.
2. Place the pastry circle on the pie dish and press out any air trapped underneath. Trim the edge with a knife.
3. Roll out the pastry that is left and cut four strips about ½ inch (1 centimetre) wide and long enough to go right across the pie dish. Leave these on one side.
4. Mix together the syrup, lemon juice and bread crumbs in the bowl.
5. Fill the pie with this mixture.
6. Use the strips of pastry to make a criss-cross pattern across the pie, wetting the ends with water to stick them to

the edge of the pie. Then decorate the edge with a knife handle or spoon.

7. Bake in a hot oven (Electric 400 °F., Gas 6) for about 30 minutes.

Baked egg custard *

What you need

Rolled out short crust pastry
2 eggs
1 pint (560 millilitres) milk
1 ounce (30 grammes) sugar
Pinch of grated nutmeg
Deep pie dish
Knife and fork
Mixing bowl

What to do

1. Roll out the pastry until the piece is large enough to line the pie dish.
2. Place the pastry in the pie dish and press out any air trapped underneath. Trim the edges neatly with a knife.
3. Put the eggs and sugar into the mixing bowl and beat them together with the fork.
4. Add the milk to this mixture.
5. Pour this mixture into the pie dish, leaving at least $\frac{1}{2}$ inch (1 centimetre) of pastry above the level of the filling.

6. Sprinkle a little grated nutmeg on the top.
7. Bake in a moderate oven (Electric 350 °F., Gas 4) for about 30 minutes, until the custard has turned solid and has a golden brown skin on top.
8. Leave to cool before serving.

Rough puff pastry ★★

(This is more difficult to make than short crust pastry so get lots of practice with short crust before you try to make rough puff. When you are ready to try, follow the instructions very carefully, and leave yourself plenty of time, two hours if possible, to make this kind of pastry.)

What you need

8 ounces (225 grammes) plain flour
6 ounces (170 grammes) butter
2 teaspoonfuls lemon juice
4 tablespoonfuls cold water
Mixing bowl and wooden spoon, sieve
Rolling board and pin
Knife

What to do

1. Sieve the flour into a mixing bowl.
2. Cut the butter into small pieces and mix with the flour.
3. Add the lemon juice and enough water to make a soft dough. Don't let it get sticky and don't break up the pieces of butter.
4. Flour the board and roll out the dough into a long strip.
5. Fold the strip of dough into three.
6. Turn the folded dough round so that the folded edges are at the sides.
7. Roll the dough out again into a strip.

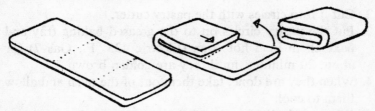

8. Fold the strip into three again and then leave it to rest for about 30 minutes in a refrigerator or a very cool place.
9. Roll out the dough again into a strip and fold it into three again. Turn it so that the folded edges are at the sides and roll out again and fold it into three. Leave for another 30 minutes in the refrigerator or a very cool place.
10. Finally roll out the dough until it is about ⅛ inch (3 millimetres) thick. Now it is ready to cut into shape to use in the following recipes.

Cream puffs **

What you need

Rough puff pastry
¼ pint (140 millilitres) double cream
Raspberry jam
Icing sugar
Flat baking tray
Rolling board and pin
Mixing bowl
Whisk or large fork
Round pastry cutter about 2½ inches (6 centimetres) across
Knife and spoon

What to do

1. Roll out the pastry until just over ½ inch (1 centimetre) thick.

2. Cut it into circles with the pastry cutter.

3. Put the pastry circles on to the greased baking tray and bake them in a hot oven (Electric 425 °F., Gas 7) for about 20 minutes, until they are golden brown.

4. When they are done, take them out of the oven and allow them to cool.

5. When cool, slit them carefully in two.

6. Spread some jam on the bottom half of each puff.

7. Whisk the cream in the bowl until it is stiff and spread cream on the top half of each puff.

8. Sandwich the two halves together.

9. Dust the top of each puff with a little icing sugar.

Cream slices **

What you need

Rough puff pastry
¼ pint (140 millilitres) double cream
Raspberry jam
2 ounces (55 grammes) icing sugar
Cup of water
Flat baking tray
Rolling board and pin
Two small mixing bowls
Whisk or large fork
Knife and spoon
Sieve

What to do

1. Roll out the pastry until it is just over ½ inch (1 centimetre) thick.

2. Cut the pastry into oblong shapes about 4 inches (10 centimetres) long and 1 inch (3 centimetres) wide.

3. Put the pastry slices on to the baking tray and bake them

in a hot oven (Electric 425 °F., Gas 7) for about 20
minutes until golden brown.

4. When they are done, take them out of the oven and allow
   them to cool.
5. When they are cool, slit them carefully in two.
6. Spread jam on the bottom half of each slice.
7. Whisk the cream in a bowl until it is stiff and spread
   cream on the top half of each slice.
8. Sandwich the two halves together.
9. Sieve the icing sugar into a bowl and mix with just enough
   water to make a paste which will spread easily.
10. Finish the slices off by spreading a thin layer of icing on
    top of each one. Allow the icing to set before eating.
    (You can colour and flavour the icing if you wish—see
    the recipe for different kinds of icing on page 47.)

Eccles cakes **

What you need

Rough puff pastry
2 ounces (55 grammes) currants
1 ounce (30 grammes) chopped candied peel
½ ounce (15 grammes) butter or margarine
½ ounce (15 grammes) sugar
Milk and a pastry brush
Pinch of mixed spice
Pinch of grated nutmeg
Flat baking tray
Rolling board and pin
Large pastry cutter about 4 inches across
Small mixing bowl
Knife and spoon

What to do

1. Roll out the pastry until it is about ¼ inch (6 millimetres) thick.
2. Cut it into circles about 4 inches (10 centimetres) across.
3. Mix the butter and sugar together in the bowl until they are creamy.
4. Add to this mixture the currants, peel and spices.
5. Put a large teaspoonful of this mixture into the centre of each circle of pastry.
6. Turn the edges of the pastry in until the fruit mixture is wrapped up in a parcel and press the edges together firmly. The whole thing should now look like a little round flat cake.
7. Turn the cakes over and roll each of them gently until the currants begin to show through the pastry.
8. Make two little slits in the top of each cake.
9. Brush the top of each cake with a little milk.
10. Put the cakes on the tray and bake in a hot oven (Electric 425 °F., Gas 7) for about 20 minutes until golden brown.

Cornish pasties — for 4 people ★★★

What you need

Rough puff pastry
6 ounces (170 grammes) raw minced beef
6 ounces (170 grammes) potatoes
1 small onion
Pinch of salt and pepper
A little water
Flat baking tray
Rolling board and pin
Small mixing bowl
Sharp knife and chopping board

What to do

1. Wash and peel the potatoes and skin the onion and chop them all into small pieces.
2. Put the chopped vegetables in the mixing bowl with the meat and add just enough water to make the mixture stick together.
3. Add salt and pepper.
4. Divide the mixture into four equal parts.
5. Divide the pastry into four equal pieces and roll them into circles about $\frac{1}{4}$ inch (6 millimetres) thick.
6. Place a quarter of the meat mixture in the centre of each pastry circle.
7. Wet the edges of the pastry with water.
8. Fold the pastry over so that it covers the meat mixture and press the edges together firmly.
9. Decorate the pastry edges with the handle of a knife or spoon.
10. Put the pasties on the baking tray and bake in a hot oven for 10 minutes (Electric 400 °F., Gas 6).
11. Reduce the oven heat to Electric 300 °F., Gas 3, and bake for another 50 minutes.

Meat patties ★★★

What you need

Rough puff pastry
6 ounces (170 grammes) raw minced beef
1 small onion
Pinch of salt and pepper
A little water
Patty pans
Rolling board and pin
Small mixing board

Knife and chopping board
2 pastry cutters, one 2½ inches (6 centimetres) and one 1½
   inches (4 centimetres) across
Spoon

   What to do

1. Skin the onion and chop it into small pieces.
2. Mix the chopped onion with the meat, salt and pepper
   and enough water to make the mixture stick together.
3. Roll the pastry to about ⅛ inch (3 millimetres) thick.
4. Cut one large and one small circle of pastry for each
   patty pan.
5. Put the large circles of pastry into the patty pans and
   press them down well so that they fit neatly.
6. Fill each patty with a spoonful of meat mixture.
7. Moisten the edges of the large circles with a little water.
8. Put a small circle of pastry on to the top of the meat and
   seal the edge firmly to the lower circle to close up the
   patty.
9. With the point of a knife make a small slit in the top of
   each patty.
10. Bake the patties in a hot oven (Electric 400 °F., Gas 6)
    for about 45 minutes.

Chapter 5

HOW TO MAKE BISCUITS

Plain biscuits *

What you need

8 ounces (225 grammes) plain flour
4 ounces (110 grammes) butter or margarine
3 ounces (85 grammes) caster sugar
1 small egg
$\frac{1}{2}$ teaspoonful lemon or vanilla essence
Mixing bowl
Fork or wooden spoon
Rolling board and pin
Flat baking tray
Pastry cutter about $2\frac{1}{2}$ inches (6 centimetres) across

What to do

1. Put the butter and sugar into the mixing bowl and cream them together with a fork or spoon until they are light in colour and fluffy.
2. Add the egg and beat the mixture well.
3. Add the flavouring essence and mix in.
4. Add the flour to the mixture a little at a time and mix well.
5. Pick up the mixture and knead it in your hands into a smooth ball.
6. Roll out the mixture to about $\frac{1}{8}$ inch (3 millimetres) thick and prick it all over with a fork.

7. Cut into circles with the pastry cutter and arrange on the baking tray.
8. Bake in a moderate oven (Electric 350 °F., Gas 4) for about 15 minutes until pale brown in colour.

You can use this plain biscuit mixture to make fancy biscuits.

Shrewsbury biscuits *

What you need

Plain biscuit mixture
2 ounces (50 grammes) currants
Icing sugar

What to do

1. Use the same recipe as for plain biscuits but add the currants at the same time as the flour.
2. Roll out the dough to about $\frac{1}{8}$ inch (3 millimetres) thick and prick it all over with a fork.
3. Cut into rounds with a pastry cutter OR into crescents by using the cutter half-way across the edge of the rolled out dough.
4. Arrange on the baking tray and bake in a moderate oven (Electric 350 °F., Gas 4) for about 15 minutes.
5. Sprinkle with a little icing sugar while still warm.

Iced biscuits *

What you need

Plain biscuit mixture
4 ounces (110 grammes) icing sugar
1 tablespoonful lukewarm water
Flavourings: lemon, raspberry, orange, coffee etc.
Colourings: yellow, pink, orange etc.
Sieve
Mixing bowl and 2 or 3 small bowls or cups
Spoon
Knife

What to do

1. Make a plain biscuit mixture and roll it out thinly.
2. Cut the dough into different shapes with a pastry cutter and a knife—circles, oblongs, squares, crescents etc.
3. Put the shapes on to the baking tray and bake in a moderate oven (Electric 350 °F., Gas 4) for about 15 minutes.
4. Leave the biscuits to cool on a wire tray or plate.
5. Sieve the icing sugar into the mixing bowl.
6. Add the water a little at a time and stir it in thoroughly until the icing is smooth and as stiff as thick cream.
7. Divide the icing into portions in separate bowls or cups, one for each colour you want to make.
8. Add the flavourings and colourings: for example—leave one portion of icing white; add raspberry flavouring and pink colouring to another; add orange flavour and colouring to another; or lemon flavour and yellow colouring to another; or coffee essence to another. (Coffee and cocoa *powders* are not suitable for flavouring icing because they do not mix smoothly.)

9. Beat each separate bowl of icing with a clean spoon until smooth and glossy.
10. Spread icing on one side of each biscuit with a knife and leave to set hard.

Jumbles *

What you need

Plain biscuit mixture
Caster sugar
Mixed nuts and/or sultanas

What to do

1. Make the plain biscuit mixture and divide the dough into pieces about the size of the bowl of a teaspoon.
2. Roll each piece in the hands into a thin sausage shape, using caster sugar on the fingers if the mixture is at all sticky.
3. Make fancy shapes with the sausage-shaped biscuits: circles, zig-zags and the letter S, making sure to join the ends up firmly where necessary. Why not make the initial letters of your family names?
4. Decorate each shape with a nut or a sultana and bake like plain biscuits.

Shortbread *

What you need

4 ounces (110 grammes) plain flour
2 ounces (55 grammes) caster sugar
2 ounces (55 grammes) rice flour (use extra 2 ounces (55 grammes) plain flour if not available)
4 ounces (110 grammes) butter
Sieve

Mixing bowl
Rolling board and pin
Flat baking tray
Fork

What to do

1. Sieve the flour, rice flour and sugar into the mixing bowl.
2. Cut the butter into small pieces and rub it into the mixture with your fingers.
3. Knead the mixture well with your fingers until it sticks together in a good thick dough.
4. *Either* roll the mixture out to about ¼ inch (6 millimetres) thick and cut into oblong shapes *or* make the mixture into a round flat cake.
5. Prick the top of the shortbread all over with a fork.
6. Arrange the shortbread on the baking tray and if you have made one large cake mark the top in slices with a knife.
7. Bake in a moderate oven (Electric 380 °F., Gas 5) until it is beginning to turn brown.
8. Turn the oven down to Electric 300 °F., Gas 3, and allow the shortbread to bake for an hour altogether.

Ginger biscuits *

What you need

4 ounces (110 grammes) plain flour
2 ounces (55 grammes) margarine
2 tablespoonfuls golden syrup
1 ounce (30 grammes) sugar
1 level teaspoonful ground ginger
½ level teaspoonful bicarbonate of soda
Mixing bowl and wooden spoon
Knife
Flat baking tray

D

What to do

1. Put the flour into the mixing bowl.
2. Chop the margarine into small pieces and add to the flour.
3. Rub the flour and margarine together with your fingertips until it looks like fine bread crumbs.
4. Add the sugar, ginger and bicarbonate of soda and mix in.
5. Add the syrup and mix to a stiff dough with a wooden spoon. If the mixture is too dry add a few drops of water.
6. Divide the dough into 18 or 20 small pieces.
7. Roll each piece into a ball in the hands and place well apart on the baking tray.
8. Bake in a moderate oven (Electric 350 °F., Gas 4) for 15 to 20 minutes until rich brown in colour.

Gingerbread men *

What you need

Ginger biscuit dough (made according to the previous recipe)
Currants and sultanas
Glacé cherries and angelica
Rolling board and pin
A little flour
Greaseproof paper
Sharp knife
Palette knife

What to do

1. Make a pattern for a gingerbread man by cutting it out of greaseproof paper—he should have short stubby arms and legs and a big round head. (See the pattern on the right.)
2. Roll out the ginger biscuit dough to about ⅛ inch (3 millimetres) thick, using plenty of flour to stop it sticking to the board or the rolling pin.

3. Put the pattern on to the dough and cut round it carefully with a knife. Repeat this until all the dough is used up and you have several gingerbread men.
4. Lift the gingerbread men carefully on to the greased baking tray with the palette knife, spacing them out well on the tray.
5. Stick three currants on to the face for eyes and nose, three sultanas on the body for buttons, a slice of cherry for a mouth and a piece of angelica for a bow tie.
6. Bake in a moderate oven (Electric 330 °F., Gas 3) until rich brown in colour.

Brandy snaps **

What you need

2½ ounces (70 grammes) sugar
1 ounce (30 grammes) butter or margarine
1 tablespoonful golden syrup
1 ounce (30 grammes) plain flour
1 level teaspoonful ground ginger
Mixing bowl and wooden spoon
Flat baking tray
Knife

What to do

1. Cream the sugar and butter together with a fork or spoon in the mixing bowl until light and fluffy.
2. Add the syrup, flour and ginger and mix thoroughly.
3. Put teaspoonfuls of the mixture on to the greased baking tray, spacing them well apart because the mixture spreads when cooking.
4. Bake in a cool oven (Electric 310 °F., Gas 2½) for about 10 minutes until a rich brown colour.
5. Allow to cool slightly.

6. Lift carefully from the baking tray with a knife and roll each brandy snap around the handle of a wooden spoon. The brandy snaps will quickly harden in this rolled up shape.
7. The brandy snaps can be filled with whipped cream when they are cold, or can be eaten as they are.

Oat crunches *

What you need

2 ounces (55 grammes) self-raising flour
2 ounces (55 grammes) oatmeal or rolled oats
1 ounce (30 grammes) margarine
1 ounce (30 grammes) sugar
A little milk
Mixing bowl and wooden spoon
Flat baking tray

What to do

1. Cream the sugar and margarine with a spoon or fork in the mixing bowl until light and fluffy.
2. Add the flour and oatmeal and beat well with the wooden spoon.
3. Add just enough milk to make a very stiff dough.
4. Spoon into small heaps on the greased baking tray.
5. Bake in a moderate oven (Electric 380 °F., Gas 5) for about 20 minutes.

Chapter 6

HOW TO MAKE SCONES AND CAKES

Plain scones *

What you need

8 ounces (225 grammes) self-raising flour
3 ounces (85 grammes) lard or margarine
2 ounces (55 grammes) sugar
A good pinch salt
¼ pint (140 millilitres) milk
Mixing bowl and wooden spoon
Rolling board and pin
Pastry cutter about 2½ inches (6 centimetres) across
Flat baking tray

What to do

1. Put the flour and salt into the mixing bowl.
2. Chop the fat into small pieces and rub them into the flour with your fingers until the mixture is like fine bread crumbs.
3. Mix in the sugar.
4. Add all the milk and mix quickly but very lightly to a spongy dough.
5. Knead the dough together very lightly with your hands.
6. Roll it out lightly to about ¾ inch (2 centimetres) thick.
7. Cut into circles with the pastry cutter and arrange on the tray.

8. Brush the tops of the scones with milk and put them in the oven.
9. Bake in a hot oven (Electric 425 °F., Gas 7) for 10 minutes. You can also make a ring of scones with this mixture: shape the dough into a flat cake and mark the top with a deep cross with a knife. Bake at the same heat but for 5 or 10 minutes longer than the small scones.

Cheese scones *

What to do

Follow the recipe for plain scones but leave out the sugar and add 3 ounces (85 grammes) of grated cheese to the recipe. Add the cheese to the mixture at the same time as the flour.

Currant scones *

What to do

Add 2 ounces (55 grammes) washed currants to the recipe for plain scones. Put the fruit into the mixture at the same time as the flour.

Scotch pancakes **

What you need

8 ounces (225 grammes) self-raising flour
A good pinch salt
1 egg
1 tablespoonful sugar
½ pint (280 millilitres) milk
A little lard or suet
Mixing bowl and wooden spoon
Griddle or smooth electric hotplate or heavy iron frying pan
Cup

Dessertspoon
Broad knife or fishslice

What to do

1. Put the flour and salt into the mixing bowl.
2. Break the egg into a cup.
3. Make a well in the centre of the flour and pour in the egg and a little of the milk.
4. Mix with the wooden spoon and add more milk to make a batter like thick cream.
5. Add the sugar and mix.
6. Heat the griddle (or hotplate or frying pan) and grease it carefully with a little lard or suet.
7. Put a dessertspoonful of the mixture on to the hot griddle to make a small pancake.
8. When bubbles rise to the surface of the pancake turn it over with the knife to brown it on the other side. Repeat until all the batter has been used up.
9. Cool the pancakes on a clean tea-towel and serve with butter.

Potato scones ★★

What you need

8 ounces (225 grammes) cold cooked potatoes
½ ounce (15 grammes) margarine
Pinch of salt
About 3 ounces (85 grammes) plain flour
A little lard or suet
Mixing bowl
Small saucepan
Potato masher or large fork
Rolling pin and board
Pastry cutter 3½ inches (9 centimetres) across

Griddle (or smooth electric hotplate or heavy iron frying pan)
Palette knife or wide, broad-bladed knife

What to do

1. Mash the potatoes smoothly.
2. Melt the margarine in the pan and add it to the potatoes.
3. Add as much salt to the mixture as necessary. Taste to make sure.
4. Use your fingers to work in as much flour as the mixture will take. It may not need the whole 3 ounces (85 grammes).
5. Roll the dough out thinly.
6. Cut into circles with the pastry cutter and prick with a fork.
7. Heat the griddle and grease it with a little lard or suet.
8. Place the scones on the hot griddle and cook for about 3 minutes on each side until golden brown.

Sponge cake ★★

What you need

3 eggs
4 ounces (110 grammes) caster sugar
4 ounces (110 grammes) self-raising flour
Cake tin 6 or 7 inches (between 15 and 20 centimetres) across
A little oil
Mixing bowl
Whisk or large fork
Sieve
Spoon
Pan of hot, not boiling, water

What to do

1. Grease the cake tin with the oil.
2. Mix 1 teaspoonful sugar and 1 teaspoonful flour together

and sprinkle over the inside of the tin until it is well covered.
3. Put the eggs and sugar into the mixing bowl.
4. Put the bowl over the pan of hot, not boiling, water, making sure that it does not touch the water, and whisk the eggs and sugar until they are very thick and creamy. This may take 15 minutes or more.
5. Sieve the flour and fold it very gently into the mixture.
6. Pour the mixture into the cake tin and sprinkle a little sugar on top.
7. Bake in a moderate oven (Electric 380 °F., Gas 5) for about 25 minutes. Test the cake to make sure it is done before you take it out of the oven. It should be golden brown on top and when pressed in the centre with a spoon or the blade of a knife it should rise back into shape.

Sponge sandwich ★★

What to do

1. Make a sponge cake according to the previous recipe.
2. Allow the cake to cool, then slit it in two with a sharp knife.
3. Spread the bottom half with jam, whipped cream, butter cream (see recipe below) or jam and whipped cream.
4. Replace the top of the sandwich and sprinkle with icing sugar.

Iced sponge ★★

What to do

1. Make a sponge cake according to the recipe on page 57.
2. Allow the cake to cool, slit it in two and sandwich it with jam or cream.

3. Make plain or flavoured icing, according to the recipe on page 47 and spread it on the top of the cake with a broad knife. Allow the icing to set hard before serving.

Butter cream ★

What you need

4 ounces (110 grammes) butter
4 ounces (110 grammes) icing sugar
Sieve
Mixing bowl
Whisk or large fork

What to do

1. Put the butter into the mixing bowl and sieve in the icing sugar.
2. Cream the butter and sugar together and then beat very thoroughly until the mixture is smooth and light.

Butter cream can be flavoured with coffee essence, a teaspoonful of cocoa powder or fruit flavourings.

Small sponge cakes ★★

What you need

Sponge cake mixture made according to the recipe on page 57
Patty pans
Oil
Spoon
1 teaspoonful of flour and sugar mixed

What to do

1. Grease all the patty pans with oil.
2. Sprinkle the flour and sugar mixture into all the patty pans to cover the oiled surface.

3. Put a spoonful of sponge mixture into each patty pan and sprinkle a little sugar on top.
4. Bake in a hot oven (Electric 400 °F., Gas 6) for about 10 minutes until they are firm and brown.
5. Allow to cool, then either split them and fill them with jam and cream or ice them, using the recipe for icing on page 47.

Swiss roll ★★★

What you need

3 eggs
4 ounces (110 grammes) caster sugar
3 ounces (85 grammes) self-raising flour
½ teaspoonful vanilla essence
1 or 2 tablespoonfuls warm water
2 tablespoonfuls jam
Swiss roll tin 12 inches by 9 inches (30 centimetres by 23 centimetres)
Mixing bowl
Whisk or large fork
Spoon and knife
Greaseproof paper
Oil
A little sugar
Pan of hot, not boiling, water
Clean tea-towel

What to do

1. Grease the tin and line it with greaseproof paper, well smoothed down.
2. Put the eggs and sugar into the mixing bowl.
3. Put the bowl over the pan of hot water, making sure that

it does not touch the water, and whisk the mixture until it is very thick and creamy.

4. Add the vanilla essence.
5. Sieve the flour into the mixture and fold it in very gently.
6. Add just enough warm water to make the mixture thin enough to pour easily.
7. Pour the mixture into the tin making sure that it runs into all the corners.
8. Bake in a hot oven (Electric 450 °F., Gas 8) for 7 to 10 minutes until it is firm and light brown in colour.
9. Spread a sheet of greaseproof paper out flat and sprinkle it with sugar.
10. Turn the roll on to the sugared paper and cover with a clean tea-towel. Allow it to cool slightly but do not let it go cold.
11. Warm the jam.
12. When the roll has cooled slightly, cut off the edges if they have baked crisp or dark brown and throw them away.
13. While the roll is still warm, spread it with warm jam.
14. Now roll it up carefully—Begin by bending the long edge farthest from you in about ½ inch (1 centimetre) and press it over firmly. Then put your hands palm down on to

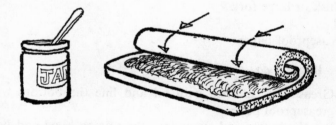

this turned edge and roll the whole thing towards you. If you roll it gently enough the cake will not crack as it is rolled up.

Chocolate roll ★★★

What to do

Add 3 teaspoonfuls cocoa powder to the recipe for Swiss roll.

Add the cocoa at the same time as the flour. You will also need a little extra warm water to make a pouring mixture.

Fill the roll with chocolate-flavoured butter cream (see the recipe on page 59) instead of jam. Roll it up in the same way as a Swiss roll.

Victoria sandwich ★

What you need

4 ounces (110 grammes) butter or margarine
4 ounces (110 grammes) caster sugar
4 ounces (110 grammes) self-raising flour
2 eggs
Pinch of salt
Sandwich cake tin about 7 inches (17 centimetres) across
2 mixing bowls and a wooden spoon
Whisk or large fork
Oil
Greaseproof paper

What to do

1. Grease the cake tin with oil and line the bottom with greaseproof paper.
2. Put the butter and sugar into the mixing bowl and beat them with a spoon or fork until they turn pale in colour and look fluffy.
3. Whisk the eggs in a separate bowl.

4. Add a little of the egg to the butter mixture and mix together thoroughly. Repeat this until all the egg has been used up.
5. Add the flour and salt to the mixture and stir gently.
6. Pour the mixture into the cake tin.
7. Bake in a moderate oven (Electric 350 °F., Gas 4) for about 45 minutes.

Fillings and icings

1. Allow the cake to cool then slit it in two with a sharp knife.
2. Spread the bottom half of the cake with either jam, or whipped cream or butter cream (see recipe on page 59) or with jam and cream.
3. Replace the top of the sandwich.
4. Either sprinkle the top of the cake with icing sugar, or ice it with any colour or flavour of icing, following the recipe for icing on page 47.

Chocolate cake **

What you need

$3\frac{1}{2}$ ounces (100 grammes) self-raising flour
$1\frac{1}{2}$ ounces (40 grammes) cocoa powder
Pinch of salt
4 ounces (110 grammes) butter or margarine
4 ounces (110 grammes) caster sugar
2 eggs
Chocolate butter cream (see recipe on page 59)
Cake tin about 8 inches (20 centimetres) across
Oil
Greaseproof paper
2 mixing bowls and a wooden spoon
Whisk or large fork

What to do

1. Grease the cake tin with oil and line it completely with oiled greaseproof paper.
2. Put the butter and sugar into the mixing bowl and beat them together with a fork or spoon until they turn pale in colour and look fluffy.
3. In a separate bowl, mix together the flour, cocoa and salt.
4. Add one egg and one spoonful of flour mixture to the creamed butter and sugar and beat together thoroughly. Do the same with the second egg and another spoonful of flour mixture.
5. Add the rest of the flour mixture and stir in lightly.
6. Pour the mixture into the cake tin and smooth the surface with a spoon.
7. Bake in a fairly hot oven (Electric 375 °F., Gas 5) for 30 to 35 minutes.
8. Allow the cake to cool.
9. Make chocolate butter cream according to the recipe on page 59.
10. Slit the cake in two and spread half the cream on the bottom half of the cake.
11. Replace the top of the cake to make a sandwich.
12. Spread the rest of the cream on top of the cake. Decorate it by making a pattern with a fork or with a little grated chocolate, or chocolate drops or walnuts, if you have any.

Raspberry buns *

What you need

8 ounces (225 grammes) self-raising flour
2 ounces (55 grammes) sugar
Cup of milk
3 ounces (85 grammes) butter or margarine

1 egg
Pinch of salt
Raspberry jam
Flat baking tray
2 mixing bowls
Sieve
Whisk or large fork
Wooden spoon and teaspoon
Cup of water and pastry brush

What to do

1. Sieve the flour into a mixing bowl.
2. Add the margarine and rub it into the flour with your fingers until it looks like fine bread crumbs.
3. Add the sugar and mix.
4. Whisk the egg in a separate bowl and then add it to the flour.
5. Add enough milk to make a slightly sticky mixture. You may not need the whole cupful.
6. Cut the dough into eight small pieces, dip your hands in flour and roll each piece of dough into a ball in your fingers.
7. Make a hole in the centre of each ball with your fingers and fill each hole with about ¼ teaspoonful raspberry jam.
8. Close up the balls so that the jam is completely hidden inside the dough.
9. Place the balls hole-side down on the table.
10. Brush the top of each bun with water and sprinkle evenly with sugar.
11. Lift them carefully on to the greased baking tray, spacing them evenly.
12. Bake in a hot oven (Electric 430 °F., Gas 7) for about 20 minutes.

E

Rock buns *

What you need

8 ounces (225 grammes) self-raising flour
4 ounces (110 grammes) butter or margarine
3 ounces (85 grammes) sugar
Pinch of salt
3 ounces (85 grammes) currants
1 ounce (30 grammes) candied peel
Pinch of mixed spice or nutmeg
1 egg
2 tablespoonfuls milk
Flat baking tray
2 mixing bowls and wooden spoon
Whisk or large fork

What to do

1. Put the flour, salt and butter into a mixing bowl and rub together with your fingers until it looks like fine bread crumbs.
2. Add the sugar, currants, candied peel and spice.
3. Mix the egg and milk together in a separate bowl.
4. Add the liquid to the flour mixture and mix to a smooth dough.
5. Spoon the mixture into rough heaps on the baking tray, spacing them evenly.
6. Bake in a hot oven (Electric 400 °F., Gas 6) for about 20 minutes.

Parkin **

What you need

8 ounces (225 grammes) self-raising flour
8 ounces (225 grammes) medium oatmeal

4 ounces (110 grammes) sugar
3 ounces (85 grammes) lard or margarine
8 ounces (225 grammes) golden syrup
Pinch of salt
½ teaspoonful ground ginger
¼ pint (140 millilitres) milk
Oblong baking tin about 11 inches by 9 inches and 2 inches
    deep (28 centimetres by 23 centimetres and 5 centimetres
    deep) or a round cake tin about 8 inches (20 centimetres)
    across
Oil
Greaseproof paper
Mixing bowl and wooden spoon
Small saucepan

What to do

1. Oil the baking tin and line it completely with oiled greaseproof paper.
2. Put the flour, salt, oatmeal and ginger in a bowl and mix.
3. Put the sugar, lard, syrup and half the milk in the saucepan
   and melt them over a low heat. *Do not boil.* Allow to cool
   slightly.
4. Add the melted ingredients to the flour mixture and stir in.
5. Add the rest of the milk and stir in quickly.
6. Pour into the baking tin.
7. Bake for 1 hour and 20 minutes in a cool oven (Electric
   300 °F., Gas 2). Parkin will keep for two weeks or more in
   a tin. In any case it is better to leave it for at least a day
   before slicing.

Coconut cake ★

What you need

4 ounces (110 grammes) butter or margarine

4 ounces (110 grammes) sugar
3 eggs
7 ounces (195 grammes) self-raising flour
Pinch of salt
2 ounces (55 grammes) desiccated coconut
Cake tin about 6 inches (15 centimetres) across
Mixing bowl and wooden spoon
Oil
Greaseproof paper

What to do

1. Oil the baking tin and line it completely with oiled grease-proof paper.
2. Put the butter and sugar into the mixing bowl and beat them together with a spoon or fork until they turn pale in colour and look fluffy.
3. Add the eggs to the mixture one at a time and beat them in well.
4. Add the flour, salt and coconut and stir lightly until well mixed.
5. Pour the mixture into the cake tin and bake for 1¼ hours in a moderate oven (Electric 350 °F., Gas 4).
6. If you wish, ice the cake with white icing, following the icing recipe on page 47, and decorate by sprinkling with desiccated coconut while the icing is still wet.

Chapter 7

HOW TO COOK A MEAL

When you have been cooking single dishes for a little while you will probably want to start preparing complete meals for your family. The next section of this book tells you how to do this, first by giving recipes for main dishes and puddings, by telling you how to prepare fruit and salads, and lastly advising you how to plan a menu so that you can cook a complete meal.

Do not rush

Do not rush into preparing a whole meal all at once. It is much more difficult than making just one dish at a time. So start by helping your mother to do just part of a meal: perhaps she could cook the main course while you made the pudding. Or make the main dish for tea and get some help with the cakes or sweet, or make these well in advance.

Even when you do go on to cooking a complete meal you can make things much easier for yourself by spreading out the cooking and preparation. Make a cold sweet or cakes earlier in the day and this will give you more time to concentrate on the main dishes.

Later on when you get more expert you will be able to cook everything at once.

Cooking on top of the cooker

Read again the hints on cooking on top of the cooker on

page 17. Watch your pans very carefully, especially if you are
frying or grilling, and never use a very fierce heat. A moderate
one will do the job just as well with much less danger of pans
boiling over or food burning.

Stirring

Stirring is very important with some foods that you cook on
top of the cooker, so if the recipe tells you to stir then it
really means it. Custards and puddings in saucepans need
stirring to stop them going lumpy. Meat can easily stick to
the bottom of the pan if it is not stirred. But there is no need
to stir boiling vegetables.

When is it done?

The reason for cooking meat and vegetables is simply to make
them more tender to eat so you can usually tell when they are
done by testing to see whether they are soft enough to eat
easily. Use a fork to test whether meat, fish or vegetables are
tender. If it goes to the centre easily then they are done.

How long will it take?

Meat is usually the thing which takes longest to cook—it can
take 2 or 3 hours if it is cooked in the oven. Boiling meat
makes it tender rather more quickly. This may take about
30 minutes. Quickest of all is grilling or frying which may
take only 10 or 15 minutes. So give yourself plenty of time to
make a meat dish cooked in the oven.

Vegetables too take longer when cooked in the oven: perhaps an hour for roast or baked potatoes or braised vegetables. Boiled vegetables vary in their cooking time from
about 10 minutes for a soft vegetable like marrow or tomatoes
to an hour or more for very hard vegetables like turnips. Use
a fork to test whether they are tender and take them off the

heat as soon as they are done. Vegetables are easily spoiled by overcooking.

Before you serve anything *taste* it. Use a clean spoon for this, and sample the dish to make sure that it has enough salt and pepper in (remember stock cubes have salt in them so allow for this) and whether it has been cooked long enough. This is the only way to tell whether some things are done: rice and spaghetti, for instance, must feel soft between the teeth so try them to see.

Serving

Half the secret of good cooking lies in making the dish look attractive when you take it to the table. So arrange meat and fish dishes in an attractive way on a serving dish and follow the suggestions for decoration in the recipes (it is called garnishing in cookery). With sweet dishes you can use lots of imagination with the decorations, and glacé cherries, angelica, nuts, hundreds and thousands and chocolate drops will all come in useful.

Chapter 8
MEAT DISHES

Grilled sausages and tomatoes **

What you need

2 or 3 sausages for each person
1 tomato for each person
Salt and pepper
A little butter
Grill pan and fish-slice
Sharp knife
Fork

What to do

1. Turn on the grill and allow it to get hot.
2. Put the sausages on the wire tray in the grill pan and prick the skins once with a fork.
3. Put the sausages under the hot grill and allow them to get deep brown on top.
4. Wash the tomatoes and cut them in half along the 'equator'.
5. Take the grill pan from under the grill and arrange the tomato halves on the wire tray with the sausages.
6. Sprinkle salt and pepper on each tomato and add a small knob of butter.
7. Turn the sausages over.
8. Grill the sausages and tomatoes, turning the sausages once

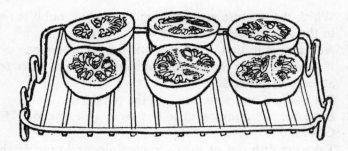

or twice, until the tomatoes are soft and the sausages are brown all round.

9. Arrange on a hot serving dish with the sausages in the centre and the tomato halves round the edge.

Toad in the hole **

What you need

4 ounces (110 grammes) plain flour
Pinch of salt
2 eggs
½ pint (280 millilitres) milk
½ pound (225 grammes) sausages
1 ounce (30 grammes) lard
Deep pie dish
Mixing bowl and wooden spoon
Whisk or large fork

What to do

1. Put the flour and salt into the mixing bowl and make a well in the centre.
2. Drop in the eggs and half the milk and mix with the whisk or fork.
3. Add the rest of the milk a little at a time, pulling the flour into the liquid gradually to make a very smooth mixture.

4. Whisk the mixture very thoroughly until air bubbles rise to the surface and burst.
5. Add any milk that is left and stir it in thoroughly.
6. If possible, leave the mixture to stand in a cool place for at least 30 minutes.
7. Put the lard and sausages into the pie dish.
8. Bake for 10 minutes in a hot oven (Electric 430 °F., Gas 7).
9. Take the dish out of the oven carefully and pour in the batter mixture.
10. Put the dish back into the oven and bake for another 30 minutes until the batter has risen and is deep golden brown and crisp on top.
11. Serve in the dish in which it has been cooked.

Grilled pork chops and apple sauce ***

What you need

1 pork chop for each person
A little oil or dripping
For the sauce: $\frac{1}{2}$ pound (225 grammes) cooking apples
              1 ounce (30 grammes) sugar
              2 teaspoonfuls water
              $\frac{1}{2}$ ounce (15 grammes) butter or margarine
Grill pan and fish-slice
Sharp knife and chopping board
Small saucepan
Sieve
Small mixing bowl and spoon
Pastry brush

What to do

1. Wash and peel the apples and slice all the flesh away from the cores.

2. Put the apple slices into the saucepan.
3. Add sugar and a dessertspoonful of water and bring to the boil over a low heat.
4. Simmer until the apples are soft, then allow them to cool.
5. Brush the chops with oil or melted dripping.
6. Place the chops on the wire tray of the grill pan.
7. Turn on the grill and allow it to get hot.
8. Put the chops under the hot grill and allow to cook for about 10 minutes until golden brown.
9. Turn the chops over and allow them to brown on the other side.
10. Pass the apples and juice through the sieve into the mixing bowl. Use the back of a spoon to push the soft flesh through the mesh of the sieve.
11. Add the butter to the apples and return the mixture to the pan.
12. Reheat the sauce gently over a low light, stirring it gently to mix in the butter as it melts.
13. Serve the chops arranged on a hot serving dish and decorated with watercress or tomato slices. Serve the sauce hot in a small bowl or jug with a spoon.

Grilled chicken with sweetcorn ★★★

What you need

1 chicken quarter for each person (allow frozen chicken to thaw before cooking)
½ ounce (15 grammes) butter for each chicken quarter
1 small tin or frozen packet of sweetcorn
Pinch of salt and pepper
Grill pan and fish-slice
Knife
Small saucepan
Colander or metal sieve

What to do

1. Take the wire tray out of the grill pan. You will not need it.
2. Put the chicken quarters into the bottom of the grill pan.
3. Put a knob of butter on top of each chicken quarter.
4. Turn on the grill and allow it to get hot.
5. Put the chicken under the grill and allow the skin on top to brown slightly.
6. Turn the grill down to a moderate heat and continue to grill the chicken, turning it over once, until it is lightly browned all over and the flesh is tender. This will take 15 to 20 minutes depending on the size of the chicken quarters.
7. While the chicken is cooking, put the sweetcorn into the saucepan and heat over a moderate light. (Follow the instructions on the packet if you are using frozen sweetcorn.)
8. Drain the liquid off the sweetcorn, using a colander or metal sieve.
9. Return the sweetcorn to the pan and add a knob of butter, salt and pepper.
10. Serve the chicken and corn together on a hot dish, the corn in the centre and the chicken quarters around it. Pour the melted butter and juices from the grill pan over the top.

Minced beef with onions — for 4 people ***

What you need

1 pound (450 grammes) minced raw beef
1 onion
½ ounce (15 grammes) dripping
Stock cube

Hot water
Pinch of salt and pepper
Frying-pan and fish-slice
Large saucepan
Knife and chopping board
Wooden spoon
Cup

What to do

1. Skin the onion and chop it into small pieces.
2. Put the dripping into the frying-pan and put the pan over a moderate heat.
3. When the dripping has melted and is hot, put the onion into the pan.
4. Fry the onions until golden brown, stirring them occasionally to stop them burning.
5. Put the minced meat and the fried onion into the saucepan.
6. Add a pinch of salt and pepper.
7. Put the stock cube into a cup of hot water and stir it until it dissolves.
8. Add the cupful of stock to the meat.
9. Bring the meat to the boil and then turn down the heat so that it simmers for about 50 minutes. Stir it occasionally to stop it sticking to the bottom of the pan.
10. Serve in a deep serving dish—if you like, surrounded by creamy mashed potato.

Spaghetti bolognese — for 4 people ★★★

What you need

½ pound (225 grammes) minced beef
1 small onion
1 tablespoonful oil

Stock cube
Hot water
1 small can tomato purée
Pinch of salt and pepper
Mixed herbs
6 ounces (170 grammes) spaghetti
2 ounces (55 grammes) grated cheese (Parmesan if possible,
    if not, hard Cheddar)
1 large and 1 medium saucepan
Knife and chopping board
Wooden spoon
Colander

What to do

1. Skin the onion and chop it into small pieces.
2. Put the oil into the small saucepan over a moderate light.
3. When the oil is hot, put the onion into the pan.
4. Fry the onion until golden brown.
5. Add the meat and stir well.
6. Add the tomato purée and a pinch of mixed herbs and stir well. Bring the pan back to the boil.
7. Put the stock cube into a cup of hot water and stir it until it dissolves.
8. Add the cupful of stock to the meat and stir well.
9. Bring the pan back to the boil, and then turn down the heat and simmer until the meat is tender.
10. Taste the meat and add pepper and as much salt as necessary.
11. While the meat is simmering, fill the large saucepan half full of water and put it over a moderate heat.
12. Add a pinch of salt.
13. When the water is boiling, break the spaghetti into pieces about 6 inches (15 centimetres) long.

14. Put the spaghetti pieces into the boiling water and bring back to the boil.
15. Turn down the heat and simmer the spaghetti for about 15 minutes. Lift a piece out carefully to taste when you think it may be done—it should be tender enough to bite through easily and should not be sticky to touch.
16. Drain the spaghetti in the colander and put it in a hot serving dish.
17. Pour the meat on top of the spaghetti and sprinkle with grated cheese.
18. Serve extra grated cheese in a small dish with a spoon on the table.

Cottage pie — for 4 people ★★★

(This can be made with fresh minced meat from the butcher, or with left-over meat minced at home. Left-over mashed potatoes can also be used.)

What you need

½ pound (450 grammes) minced meat (beef or lamb)
1 onion
Pinch of salt and pepper
Tomato ketchup or sauce
Stock cube
Hot water
1½ pounds (670 grammes) uncooked potatoes or about
    1 pound (450 grammes) cooked potatoes
1 ounce (30 grammes) butter or margarine
A little milk
2 saucepans
2 mixing bowls and spoon
Deep pie dish or casserole
Knife and chopping board

Cup and spoon
Potato masher or large fork

What to do

1. If the potatoes are raw, wash and peel them and cut them into small pieces.
2. Bring a saucepan of water to the boil and add the potatoes and a pinch of salt.
3. Simmer the potatoes over a moderate heat until they are soft.
4. Drain the potatoes in a colander.
5. Put the cooked potatoes into a mixing bowl and add a knob of butter and a little milk.
6. Mash them thoroughly.
7. Skin the onion and chop it into small pieces.
8. If the meat is raw, put it into a saucepan; if cooked, into a mixing bowl.
9. Add the chopped onion, salt and pepper and a little tomato ketchup.
10. Put the stock cube into a cup of hot water and stir it until it dissolves.
11. Add the cupful of stock to the meat and stir it all together thoroughly.
12. If the meat is raw, put the pan over a moderate heat and bring to the boil. Turn the heat down and simmer for 10 minutes.
13. Put the meat mixture into the bottom of the pie dish.
14. Cover the meat with mashed potato and decorate the top by making a pattern with a fork.
15. Bake in a hot oven (Electric 400 °F., Gas 6) for about 20 minutes until the potato is golden brown and crisp on top.
16. Serve in the dish in which it was baked

Braised beef — for 4 people ***

What you need

1½ pounds (670 grammes) braising steak (ask the butcher to
    cut it into pieces for you)
1 ounce (30 grammes) dripping
Pinch of salt and pepper
2 onions
2 carrots
Stock cube
Hot water
Frying pan and fish-slice
Earthenware or iron casserole with a lid
Sharp knife and chopping board
Cup and spoon

What to do

1. Put the frying pan over a moderate heat and put in the
   dripping.
2. Let the dripping melt and get hot.
3. Put the pieces of steak into the hot dripping and fry them
   gently for a few minutes, turning them over, until they
   are light brown on all sides.
4. Lift the meat into the casserole.
5. Pour in any fat and juices left in the frying pan.
6. Skin the onions, peel the carrots and chop them all into
   slices.
7. Put the sliced vegetables into the casserole.
8. Add a pinch of salt and pepper.
9. Put the stock cube into a cup of hot water and stir until
   it has dissolved.
10. Add the cupful of stock to the meat and vegetables.
11. Put the lid on the casserole and bake it in a cool oven
    (Electric 300 °F., Gas 2) for 1 hour 30 minutes.

F

12. Either serve the meat in the dish it was cooked in, or in a hot serving dish surrounded with mashed potato. Sprinkle a little chopped parsley over the meat before serving.

Braised liver and onions — for 4 people ***

What you need

1 pound (450 grammes) lamb's liver
3 onions
Pinch of salt and pepper
1 ounce (30 grammes) dripping
Stock cube
Hot water
Frying pan and fish-slice
Earthenware or iron casserole with a lid
Sharp knife and chopping board
Cup and spoon
Kitchen paper or a clean cloth

What to do

1. Wash the liver under running water and dry it on kitchen paper or a clean cloth.
2. Put the frying pan over a moderate heat and put in the dripping.
3. Let the dripping melt and get hot.
4. Put the pieces of liver into the hot dripping and fry them gently for a few minutes, turning them over, until they are light brown on all sides.
5. Lift the liver into the casserole.
6. Skin the onions and slice them into rings.
7. Put the onion rings into the frying pan and fry them over a moderate heat until golden brown.
8. Lift the onion rings into the casserole.

9. Pour any fat and juices left in the frying pan into the casserole.
10. Add a pinch of salt and pepper.
11. Put the stock cube into a cup of hot water and stir until it has dissolved.
12. Put the cupful of stock into the casserole.
13. Put the lid on the casserole and bake in a cool oven (Electric 300 °F., Gas 2) for 1 hour 30 minutes.
14. Either serve the meat in the dish it was cooked in, or in a hot serving dish surrounded by vegetables or mashed potato.

Braised lamb chops ★★★

What you need

1 or 2 lamb chops for each person
1 onion
1 large carrot
½ turnip
2 sticks celery
1 ounce (30 grammes) dripping
Pinch of salt and pepper
Stock cube
Hot water
Frying pan and fish-slice
Earthenware or iron casserole with a lid
Cup and spoon

What to do

1. Wash and peel or skin the vegetables and chop them all into slices.
2. Put the frying pan over a moderate heat and put in the dripping.
3. Let the dripping melt and get hot.

4. Put the chops into the hot dripping and fry them gently
   for a few minutes, turning them over once, until they are
   light brown on both sides.
5. Take the chops out of the frying pan and keep them on
   one side.
6. Put the sliced vegetables into the frying pan and fry them
   gently for a few minutes, turning them over, until they
   turn golden brown.
7. Arrange the vegetables in the bottom of the casserole and
   put the chops on top of them.
8. Pour any juices left in the pan into the casserole.
9. Add a pinch of salt and pepper.
10. Put the stock cube into a cup of hot water and stir until
    it has dissolved.
11. Put the cupful of stock into the casserole.
12. Put the lid on the casserole and bake in a cool oven
    (Electric 330 °F., Gas 3) for 1 hour.
13. Either serve the meat in the dish it was cooked in, or
    arrange the chops in the centre of a hot serving dish with
    the vegetables round the edge. Pour the juice from the
    casserole over the top and decorate with a little chopped
    parsley sprinkled over the meat.

Lancashire hotpot — for 4 people ★★★

What you need

1 pound (450 grammes) best end of lamb (ask the butcher to
cut it up for you) or lamb cutlets
1 pound (450 grammes) potatoes
2 onions
2 carrots
1 tablespoonful flour
Pinch of salt and pepper
Stock cube

Hot water
Earthenware or iron casserole with a lid
Sharp knife and chopping board
Cup and spoon

What to do

1. Wash and peel or skin all the vegetables and chop into slices.
2. Mix the flour with a little salt and pepper on the chopping board.
3. Dip each piece of meat in the seasoned flour.
4. Put the meat, onions and carrots in alternate layers in the casserole.
5. Put the stock cube into a cup of hot water and stir it until it has dissolved.
6. Add the cupful of stock to the casserole.
7. Add enough hot water to come half-way up the side of the casserole.
8. Arrange the slices of potato on top of the meat and sprinkle them with salt.
9. Put the lid on the casserole and bake in a moderate oven (Electric 350 °F., Gas 4) for about 2 hours.
10. Take the lid off the casserole and continue baking until the potatoes on the top are golden brown.
11. Serve in the dish in which it was cooked. Decorate with a sprig of parsley or mint in the centre.

Irish stew — for 4 people ★★★

What you need

1 pound (450 grammes) scrag end of mutton (ask the butcher to cut it up for you)
½ pound (225 grammes) onions
2 pounds (900 grammes) potatoes

Pinch of salt and pepper
About 1 pint (560 millilitres) water
Large stew pan
Sharp knife and chopping board

What to do

1. Skin the onions and peel the potatoes and slice them all.
2. Arrange the meat, onions and *half* the potatoes in layers in the pan. Sprinkle with salt and pepper.
3. Add enough water to cover them and bring them to the boil over a moderate heat.
4. Turn down the heat and simmer gently for 1 hour 30 minutes.
5. Put the rest of the potato slices on top of the stew and simmer for another 45 minutes until the potatoes are soft.
6. Serve the meat in the centre of a hot serving dish, surrounded by the potato slices. Decorate with a sprig of parsley.

Fried liver and bacon — for 4 people ∗∗

What you need

¾ pound (335 grammes) liver
4 rashers bacon
2 teaspoonfuls flour
Pinch of salt and pepper
½ pint (280 millilitres) water
Large frying pan and fish-slice
Sharp knife and chopping board
Wooden spoon
Kitchen paper or a clean cloth

What to do

1. Cut the rind off the bacon

2. Wash the liver under running water and dry it on kitchen paper or a clean cloth.
3. Cut the liver into slices about $\frac{1}{2}$ inch thick.
4. Put the frying pan over a moderate heat and fry the bacon until crisp.
5. Take the bacon out of the pan and keep hot until needed.
6. Fry the liver in the bacon fat left in the pan for about 5 minutes, turning it over once, until brown on each side.
7. Put the liver into a hot serving dish and arrange the bacon on top. Keep hot until needed.
8. Stir the flour into the fat left in the frying pan and brown it.
9. When the flour has turned brown, add the water, and a pinch of salt and pepper and stir well, to make gravy.
10. Allow the mixture to boil for about 4 minutes, stirring occasionally.
11. Pour the gravy around the liver in the serving dish and serve immediately.

Chapter 9

FISH DISHES

Baked fish ★★

What you need

1 fillet or steak of white fish for each person (fresh or frozen)
A little flour
Pinch of salt and pepper
Small lemon
Kitchen paper or a clean cloth
Shallow baking dish
Greaseproof paper
Chopping board
Cup

What to do

1. Wash the fish fillets under a running tap and dry on kitchen paper or a clean cloth. (There is no need to wash frozen fish or to thaw it before cooking.)
2. Mix a little flour with salt and pepper on the board.
3. Dip the fish into the flour so that it is completely coated.
4. Cut the lemon in two and squeeze the juice from one half into a cup.
5. Sprinkle lemon juice on each piece of fish.
6. Wrap each piece of fish in a piece of greaseproof paper, making a small parcel which cannot come undone easily.
7. Place the parcels of fish in the baking dish.

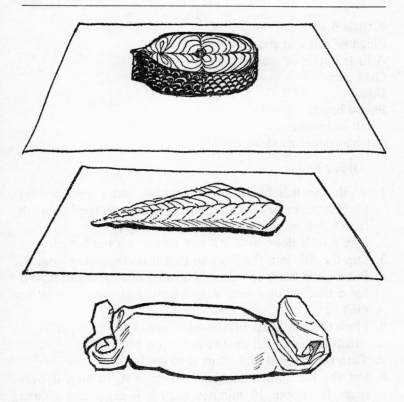

8. Bake in a moderate oven (Electric 380 °F., Gas 5) for about 20 minutes for a thin fillet or 30 to 40 minutes for a thick steak.

9. Unwrap the fillets and arrange them on a hot serving dish. Decorate with sprigs of parsley and lemon slices cut from the other half of the lemon.

Grilled fish **

What you need

1 fillet or steak of white fish for each person (fresh or frozen)

A little flour
Pinch of salt and pepper
A little butter or margarine
Grill pan
Board
Pastry brush
Small saucepan
Kitchen paper or clean cloth

What to do

1. Wash the fish fillets under running water and dry on kitchen paper or a clean cloth. (There is no need to wash frozen fish or to thaw it before cooking.)
2. Mix a little flour with salt and pepper on the board.
3. Dip the fish into the flour so that it is completely coated.
4. Put a good knob of butter in a small saucepan and heat it for a few minutes over a low light, just long enough to melt it.
5. Place the fish fillets on the wire tray of the grill pan.
6. Brush the fish with melted butter on both sides.
7. Turn on the grill and allow it to get hot.
8. Put the fish under the grill and cook it, turning it over once, for about 10 minutes until it is crisp and golden brown on both sides.
9. Place on a hot serving dish and decorate with small knobs of butter and sprigs of parsley.

Fish pie — for 4 people ★★★
This is a useful way to use up left-over fish and potato)

What you need

½ pound (225 grammes) cooked fish
½ pound (450 grammes) boiled potatoes
A little milk

Lemon juice
Pinch of salt and pepper
A little butter or margarine
Parsley
Deep pie dish
Sharp knife and chopping board
Potato masher or large fork
Wooden spoon and mixing bowl

What to do

1. Break the cooked fish up into flakes and throw away any bones or skin.
2. Chop up a good sprig of parsley as finely as possible.
3. Put the fish, parsley, salt and pepper and a knob of butter into the mixing bowl.
4. Add a squeeze of lemon juice and just enough milk to make a moist mixture. Stir together thoroughly.
5. Put the fish mixture in the bottom of the pie dish.
6. Mash the boiled potatoes with a knob of butter and a little milk and salt and pepper.
7. Put the mashed potato on top of the fish, smooth it down and decorate the top with a fork.
8. Bake the pie in a hot oven (Electric 400 °F., Gas 6) for about 30 minutes until it is brown on top.
9. Sprinkle with more chopped parsley and serve.

Fish cakes — for 4 people ★★★
(This is another way to use cooked fish and potatoes)

What you need

½ pound (225 grammes) cooked fish
½ pound (225 grammes) boiled potatoes
1 ounce (30 grammes) butter or margarine
Pinch of salt and pepper

1 egg
A little milk
Parsley
Frying pan
Oil or butter for frying
1 large and 1 small mixing bowl
Whisk or large fork
Wooden spoon

What to do

1. Break the cooked fish into small pieces, and throw away any bones or skin.
2. Mash the potatoes with a knob of butter and a little milk.
3. Chop up a good sprig of parsley as finely as possible.
4. Break the egg into a small bowl and beat it.
5. Put the fish, potatoes, salt and pepper and parsley in a large bowl and mix them together.
6. Add enough beaten egg to make the mixture stick together.
7. Divide the mixture into four and make it into round flat cakes.
8. Dust the cakes with flour so that they are completely covered.
9. Put a little oil or butter into the frying pan and heat it over a moderate heat.
10. Put the fish cakes into the hot fat and fry them on both sides until they are crisp and golden brown.
11. Serve on a hot serving dish and decorate with a small sprig of parsley.

Chapter 10

EGG AND CHEESE DISHES

Boiled eggs *

What you need

1 or 2 eggs for each person
Saucepan of water
Spoon

What to do

1. Put the pan over a moderate heat and bring the water to the boil.
2. Turn the heat down so that the water is boiling steadily.
3. Put the eggs into the boiling water very carefully with a spoon.
4. Boil the eggs for 4 minutes for soft-boiled eggs, 7 minutes for hard-boiled. Use a clock or an egg timer to time them.

Poached eggs on toast **

What you need

1 or 2 eggs for each person
1 round of bread for each person
Butter
Salt
A little vinegar

Shallow saucepan of water
Wooden spoon
Cup

What to do

1. Toast the bread under the grill, butter it and keep it hot.
2. Half fill the saucepan with water and add a pinch of salt and a teaspoonful of vinegar.
3. Put the pan over a moderate heat and bring to the boil.
4. Turn the heat down so that the water is boiling steadily.
5. Break an egg into a cup and slide it gently into the water. Put more than one egg in at a time if there is room.
6. Keep the water boiling gently and cook the egg for about 2 minutes until the white has set.
7. Lift the egg very carefully out of the water with the wooden spoon and allow the water to drain off.
8. Put the egg on a slice of hot buttered toast and serve at once.

Scrambled eggs *

What you need

1 or 2 eggs for each person
Pinch of salt and pepper
1 tablespoonful of milk
A little butter
Small saucepan
Whisk or large fork
Mixing bowl

What to do

1. Put the saucepan over a low heat.
2. Put a knob of butter in the pan and allow it to melt.
3. Break all the eggs into the mixing bowl.

4. Add salt and pepper and the milk and whisk together thoroughly.
5. Pour the egg mixture into the hot saucepan.
6. Whisk the eggs occasionally as they are cooking with a whisk or fork until they turn solid and creamy. Do not let them cook until they are dry.
7. Serve on hot buttered toast or with bacon for breakfast.

Baked eggs with ham — for 4 people ★★

What you need

1 or 2 eggs for each person
4 ounces (110 grammes) cold cooked ham
Good sprig of parsley
Pinch of salt and pepper
A little butter
Small ovenproof bowl for each person
Sharp knife and chopping board

What to do

1. Chop the cooked ham and the parsley as finely as possible.
2. Grease the bowls thoroughly with butter.
3. Divide the ham and parsley into four.
4. Sprinkle a mixture of ham and parsley on the bottom of each bowl.
5. Break one or two eggs into each bowl to cover the ham mixture.
6. Bake in a moderate oven (Electric 380 °F., Gas 5) for about 10 minutes until the egg whites are set and the yolks are still liquid.
7. Serve in the ovenproof dishes, but remember they are very hot.

Macaroni cheese — for 4 people ★★★

What you need

4 ounces (110 grammes) macaroni
4 ounces (110 grammes) Cheddar cheese
½ ounce (15 grammes) margarine
½ ounce (15 grammes) flour
½ pint (280 millilitres) milk
Pinch of salt and pepper
1 large and 1 small saucepan
Wooden spoon
Cheese grater
Colander
Deep pie dish

What to do

1. Half fill the large saucepan with water and bring it to the boil over a moderate heat.
2. Add a pinch of salt and the macaroni.
3. Boil for about 30 minutes until the macaroni is soft.
4. While the macaroni is cooking, put the margarine into the small saucepan.
5. Put it on a low heat and melt the margarine.
6. Add the flour and stir with the wooden spoon.
7. Add the milk, a little at a time, stirring it very thoroughly each time, until all the milk is used up.
8. Let this sauce boil very gently for 5 minutes until it is thick and creamy.
9. When the macaroni is done, drain it in the colander.
10. Add the macaroni to the sauce and stir it in.
11. Add salt and pepper.
12. Grate the cheese and add three-quarters of it to the macaroni and stir it in.

13. Pour this mixture into the pie dish and sprinkle the rest of the cheese on top.
14. Either bake in a hot oven (Electric 430 °F., Gas 7) until the top is brown, or put it under a hot grill until the top is brown.
15. Serve it in the dish in which it was baked.

Welsh rarebit — for 4 people ★★

What you need

½ pound (225 grammes) Cheddar cheese
4 slices of bread
1 egg
Butter
Pinch of salt and Cayenne pepper
Grill pan
Cheese grater
Mixing bowl and wooden spoon
Cup

What to do

1. Toast the bread under the grill, butter it and keep it hot.
2. Grate the cheese into the mixing bowl.
3. Add a pinch of salt and Cayenne pepper and mix in.
4. Break the egg into the cup and mix the white and yolk together.
5. Pour the egg into the cheese mixture and stir together thoroughly.
6. Spread the mixture thickly on to the buttered toast, covering the toast right to the edges.
7. Place the rounds of toast back on the wire tray of the grill pan.
8. Turn on the grill and allow to get hot

G

9. Put the toast back under the grill and cook until the cheese is light brown and toasted on top. Serve at once.

Cauliflower cheese — for 4 people ★★★

What you need

1 cauliflower
Pinch of salt and pepper
4 ounces (110 grammes) Cheddar cheese
½ ounce (15 grammes) flour
½ ounce (15 grammes) margarine
1 large and 1 small saucepan
Ovenproof dish
Wooden spoon
Cheese grater
Ladle
Colander

What to do

1. Half fill the large pan with water and bring to the boil over a moderate heat.
2. Trim the outside leaves and thick stalk off the cauliflower and wash it well.
3. Put the whole cauliflower and a pinch of salt into the boiling water carefully, and cook it until the thickest parts of the stalk are tender.
4. While the cauliflower is cooking, grate the cheese.
5. Put the margarine in the small saucepan over a low heat and let it melt.
6. Add the flour, salt and pepper, and stir with a wooden spoon.
7. Very carefully ladle a little of the hot cauliflower water into the small pan and stir thoroughly.

8. Go on adding cauliflower water, a little at a time, mixing well each time, until you have a creamy white sauce.
9. Let the sauce boil gently for 5 minutes.
10. Reduce the heat and add three-quarters of the cheese and stir it in. Keep the sauce hot but do not let it boil again.
11. When the cauliflower is done, drain it in the colander.
12. Let it cool slightly and then put it the right way up in the ovenproof dish.
13. Pour the sauce over the cauliflower so that it is completely coated.

14. Sprinkle the rest of the cheese on top.
15. Either bake it in a hot oven (Electric 430 °F., Gas 7) until brown on top, or put it under a hot grill until brown on top.
16. Serve it in the dish in which it was baked.

Baked cheese potatoes **

What you need

1 large potato for each person
4 ounces (110 grammes) Cheddar cheese
Pinch of salt and pepper
Butter
Flat baking tray
Sharp knife
Mixing bowl
Fork

What to do

1. Scrub the potatoes thoroughly and put them on the baking tray.
2. Prick them with a fork and sprinkle with salt.
3. Bake them in a moderate oven (Electric 350 °F., Gas 4) for 1 to 1½ hours until soft right through.
4. When they are done, let them cool slightly.
5. Slit them in two lengthways and scoop the soft potato out of its skin and put it in the mixing bowl.
6. Grate the cheese and add three-quarters of it to the potato.
7. Add salt and pepper and a knob of butter and mix it all together.
8. Fill the potato skins up again with this mixture.
9. Sprinkle the rest of the cheese on top of the filling.
10. Either return them to the baking tray and bake in a hot oven (Electric 430 °F., Gas 7) until brown on top, or put them under a hot grill until brown on top.
11. Serve on individual plates as a supper dish.

Chapter 11

HOW TO COOK VEGETABLES

Preparation is important

Always wash vegetables thoroughly under running water before you start to prepare them. Some will need scrubbing with a brush to remove all the soil from the skin. And look out for hidden dirt in the skin of celery or between the leaves of leeks.

Peel vegetables such as potatoes as thinly as you can with a potato peeler or a sharp knife, and do not forget to remove the little black eyes and spots.

New potatoes should have the skin scraped off with a knife —it will come off more easily if you soak them in cold water for 10 minutes first.

Green vegetables such as cabbage, sprouts or cauliflower should have the outer discoloured leaves taken off.

All vegetables should have their roots and very thick stalks cut off. Onions need the roots and stalks cutting off and the brown outer layers of skin removing.

Cook vegetables whole if you possibly can, but if they are too large to fit into your pan then cut them into pieces which will fit. They can be shredded or chopped into smaller pieces or mashed after they have been cooked much more easily than before.

The most common way to cook vegetables is simply to boil them in water. But this is not quite as simple as it sounds because vegetables can be spoiled and made tasteless by over-cooking. Use just enough water to cover the vegetables, no more, and always add a good pinch of salt to the water before you put the vegetables in. Then cook them just until they are tender, no longer, drain the water off, add a knob of butter and a little pepper and serve them immediately. Good vegetables should not be kept waiting!

Green vegetables

With any kind of green vegetable bring the water to the boil *before* you put the vegetables in. When the water is boiling drop the vegetables in carefully.

Root vegetables

Put these into cold salted water, put a lid on the pan and bring them to the boil over a moderate heat.

Frozen vegetables

You should always follow the instructions on the packet with frozen food, but for vegetables some of the general rules still apply: use as little water as possible and do not overcook them. When they are cooked, drain them and add butter and pepper in the same way as you would for fresh vegetables.

When are they done?

The aim of cooking vegetables is to make them just tender or soft enough to eat easily. The parts which will take the longest to soften will be the tough stalks or the thickest parts of root vegetables so these are the parts to test if you want to know whether they are done. When they have been boiling for 10 minutes or so prod the toughest part with a fork to see if it is soft. If not, keep on boiling and try again in another few minutes. As soon as the toughest parts are tender, the vegetables should be drained and prepared for the table.

If you want to speed up the cooking of tough vegetables cut them into small pieces. The bigger the piece the longer it will take to soften right through.

You do not have to boil them

Vegetables can be eaten raw, and there are other ways of cooking them apart from boiling.

In summer raw grated carrot and shredded white cabbage can be added to salads.

In winter, try cooking the vegetables in the oven with the meat. They can be delicious done this way.

Frozen vegetables can be cooked in the oven too—simply put the frozen block of vegetables in an ovenproof dish, add a pinch of salt and pepper, a good knob of butter, put a lid on and bake for about 10 minutes until the vegetables are tender.

Now here are some interesting vegetable recipes:

Roast potatoes *

What you need

2 or 3 medium potatoes for each person
Dripping or oil
Roasting tin
Sharp knife

What to do

1. Wash and peel the potatoes and cut them in half.
2. If meat is being roasted in the oven, put the potatoes into the tin and let them roast with the meat for about an hour until they are soft and brown on the outside.
3. If you want to cook roast potatoes separately, put a tablespoon of dripping or oil into a roasting tin.

4. Heat the tin in the oven until the fat is hot.
5. Put the potatoes into the hot fat, spoon fat over them and roast for about 1 hour in a hot oven (Electric 430 °F., Gas 7).
6. Serve in a hot serving dish.

Baked potatoes *

What you need

1 very large potato for each person
Salt
Flat baking tray
Fork
Kitchen paper or a clean cloth

What to do

1. Scrub the potatoes thoroughly under running water and dry them on kitchen paper or a clean cloth.
2. Prick the potatoes with a fork and sprinkle them with salt.
3. Place them on the baking tray and bake them in a moderate oven (Electric 350 °F., Gas 4) for 1 to 1½ hours until soft right through.

Creamed potatoes **

What you need

2 or 3 medium potatoes for each person
Butter or margarine
Potato masher or large fork
A little milk
Saucepan
Sharp knife
Colander

What to do

1. Wash and peel the potatoes and cut them into equal-sized pieces.
2. Put the potatoes in the pan.
3. Add just enough water to cover them and a pinch of salt.
4. Put the pan on a moderate heat and bring to the boil.
5. Boil the potatoes until they are soft.
6. Drain the potatoes in the colander and return them to the pan.
7. Add a large knob of butter, salt and pepper and a little milk.
8. Mash the potatoes thoroughly until they are creamy.
9. Serve in a hot dish with another knob of butter on top.

New potatoes — for 4 people ★★

What you need

1 pound (450 grammes) new potatoes
Butter or margarine
Sprigs of mint and parsley
Saucepan
Sharp knife and chopping board
Colander

What to do

1. If possible, soak the potatoes for about 10 minutes in cold water.
2. Wash the potatoes and scrape off the skin.
3. Half fill the pan with water and bring it to the boil over a moderate heat.
4. Add a pinch of salt, the sprig of mint and drop in the potatoes very carefully.
5. Boil until the potatoes are tender.

6. Drain them in the colander and return them to the pan.
7. Add a large knob of butter, salt and pepper.
8. Chop up the parsley as finely as possible.
9. Put the buttered potatoes into a hot serving dish and sprinkle them with chopped parsley.

French beans — for 4 people **

What you need

1 pound (450 grammes) French beans
Butter or margarine
Pinch of salt
Large saucepan
Sharp knife and chopping board
Colander

What to do

1. Wash the beans, then cut off the two ends and pull off as much stringy fibre from the sides as you can.
2. If the beans are small enough to fit in the pan leave them whole; if not cut them across once or twice.
3. Half fill the pan with water and bring to the boil over a moderate heat.
4. Add a pinch of salt and drop in the beans carefully.
5. Boil the beans with the lid on the pan until the beans are tender.
6. Drain the beans in the colander and return them to the pan.
7. Add a good knob of butter and reheat the pan gently to melt it.
8. Put the beans into a hot serving dish and serve immediately.

Broad beans — for 4 people **

What you need

2 pounds (900 grammes) broad beans
Butter or margarine
Pinch of salt
Parsley
Saucepan
Sharp knife and chopping board
Colander

What to do

1. Shell the beans and throw away any which are discoloured in any way.
2. Half fill the pan with water and bring to the boil over a moderate heat.
3. Add a pinch of salt and drop in the beans carefully.
4. Boil the beans until they are tender.
5. Drain the beans in the colander and return them to the pan.
6. Add a good knob of butter and reheat the pan gently to melt it.
7. Chop a good sprig of parsley as finely as possible.
8. Put the buttered beans into a hot serving dish, sprinkle with chopped parsley and serve immediately.

Brussels sprouts — for 4 people **

What you need

1 pound (450 grammes) Brussels sprouts
Butter or margarine
Salt

Saucepan
Sharp knife
Colander

What to do

1. Cut the stalk end off each sprout and take away any discoloured outside leaves.
2. Make a small cross-shaped cut in the stalk end of the sprout.
3. Soak the sprouts in cold water with a teaspoonful of salt for about 10 minutes.
4. Wash the sprouts under running water.
5. Quarter fill the pan with water and bring to the boil over a moderate heat.
6. Add a pinch of salt.
7. If the sprouts are of different sizes, put the largest ones into the boiling water first, put on the lid and bring them to the boil.
8. Add the small sprouts and boil until all the sprouts are tender with the pan lid off.
9. Drain the sprouts in the colander and return them to the pan.
10. Add a good knob of butter and reheat the pan gently to melt it.
11. Put the buttered sprouts into a hot serving dish and serve immediately.

Buttered cabbage — for 4 people ★★

What you need

1 cabbage
1 ounce (30 grammes) butter or margarine
Salt and pepper
Large saucepan

Sharp knife
Colander

What to do

1. Cut across the thick stalk at the bottom of the cabbage and take away any discoloured outer leaves.
2. Wash the cabbage very thoroughly under running water.
3. Cut the whole cabbage into four quarters and trim off the thick stalks from the centre.
4. Half fill the pan with water and bring it to the boil over a moderate heat.
5. Add a good pinch of salt and put the cabbage quarters into the water.
6. Boil until the cabbage is tender.
7. Drain in the colander and use a sharp knife to chop the cabbage into shreds.
8. Return the shredded cabbage to the pan.
9. Add about an ounce (30 grammes) of butter and some pepper.
10. Reheat the pan gently to melt the butter and mix it thoroughly with the cabbage.
11. Put the cabbage into a hot serving dish and serve immediately.

Savoury red cabbage — for 4 people ★★

What you need

1 red cabbage
½ ounce (15 grammes) butter or margarine
1 slice cooked ham
A few sultanas
Pint of water
2 tablespoonfuls vinegar
Salt and pepper

1 tablespoonful sugar
Large saucepan
Sharp knife and chopping board

What to do

1. Wash the cabbage, cut it in two and then into thin strips.
2. Chop the ham into small pieces.
3. Put the chopped cabbage and ham into the pan.
4. Add ½ pint of water, the butter, sultanas and vinegar.
5. Put on a lid and stew over a low heat for about an hour.
6. When the cabbage is tender add the rest of the water, sugar, salt and pepper and mix thoroughly.
7. Bring back to the boil and simmer without the lid until almost all the liquid has boiled away.
8. Put into a hot serving dish and serve immediately. It can also be served cold, and goes well with cheese as a supper dish.

Glazed carrots — for 4 people ★★

What you need

1 pound (450 grammes) carrots
1 ounce (30 grammes) butter or margarine
Salt
Saucepan
Sharp knife
Scrubbing brush

What to do

1. Scrub the carrots under running water.
2. Peel or scrape off the skin and cut them across into circles (very small young carrots can be cooked whole).
3. Just cover the bottom of the pan with water.
4. Add the butter and a very small pinch of salt.

5. Put the carrots into the water and bring to the boil.
6. Simmer the carrots over a low heat until tender, adding a little extra water if they boil dry.
7. When the carrots are done turn up the heat and quickly boil off any water left in the pan.
8. Put the carrots into a hot serving dish and pour over the butter left in the pan. Serve immediately.

Cauliflower with white sauce — for 4 to 6 people ★★★

What you need

1 cauliflower
Salt
For the sauce: ½ ounce (15 grammes) flour
                      ½ ounce (15 grammes) butter or margarine
                      ¼ pint (140 millilitres) milk
                      Salt and pepper
Large and small saucepan
Sharp knife
Colander
Ladle

What to do

1. Half fill the large pan with water and bring it to the boil over a moderate heat.
2. Trim the outside leaves and the thick stalk off the cauliflower and wash it thoroughly.
3. Put the whole cauliflower and a pinch of salt into the boiling water carefully, and cook it until the thickest parts of the stalk are tender.
4. While the cauliflower is cooking, put the butter into the small pan over a low heat and let it melt.
5. Add the flour and a pinch of salt and pepper and stir.
6. Add the milk and stir very thoroughly.

7. Very carefully ladle a little of the hot cauliflower water into the small pan and stir very thoroughly.
8. Go on adding cauliflower water, a little at a time, stirring well each time, until you have a creamy white sauce.
9. Let the sauce boil for 5 minutes.
10. When the cauliflower is done, drain it in the colander.
11. Put the cauliflower the right way up in a hot serving dish.
12. Pour the white sauce over it and serve immediately.

There is a recipe for CAULIFLOWER CHEESE on page 98.
(CELERY, LEEKS AND VEGETABLE MARROW CAN ALSO BE BOILED AND SERVED WITH WHITE SAUCE.)

Braised celery — for 4 people ★★

What you need

1 pound (450 grammes) celery
1 ounce (30 grammes) butter or margarine
Salt and pepper
Saucepan
Earthenware or iron casserole with a lid
Sharp knife
Scrubbing brush

What to do

1. Scrub the celery under running water and cut into pieces about 6 inches long.
2. Half fill the pan with water and bring to the boil.
3. Add a pinch of salt and put the celery carefully into the boiling water.
4. Simmer over a low heat for about 10 minutes.
5. Melt the butter in the casserole either in the oven or under the grill.
6. Lift the hot celery into the casserole.

7. Sprinkle with salt and pepper and add about ½ pint hot celery water from the saucepan.
8. Put a lid on the casserole and braise in a moderate oven (Electric 380 °F., Gas 5) for about 1 hour until the celery is tender. During the cooking spoon juice over the celery several times.
9. Lift the cooked celery into a serving dish and keep hot.
10. Boil the juice rapidly for a few minutes.
11. Pour the juice over the celery and serve immediately.

(CELERY can also be boiled and served with white sauce. See the recipe for cauliflower.)

Stewed mushrooms — for 3 or 4 people ★★

What you need

½ pound (225 grammes) button mushrooms
Chives and parsley
Salt and pepper
A little milk
A little flour
½ ounce (15 grammes) butter or margarine
Small saucepan
Sharp knife and chopping board
Cup

What to do

1. Wash the mushrooms under running water.
2. Put the butter in the pan over a low heat until the butter melts.
3. Add the mushrooms, salt and pepper and stew very gently.
4. Chop a few chives and a sprig of parsley.
5. Add the chives, parsley and about a cupful of milk to the pan and bring it back to the boil.

H

6. Mix a teaspoonful of flour with two teaspoonfuls of milk to a cream in the cup.
7. Add this mixture to the pan and stir it in thoroughly.
8. Simmer until the sauce is quite thick.
9. Pour into a hot serving dish and serve immediately.

Fried mushrooms — for 3 or 4 people ★★

What you need

½ pound (225 grammes) mushrooms
Dripping, cooking oil or bacon fat
Salt and pepper
Frying pan and fish-slice
Sharp knife and chopping board

What to do

1. Wash the mushrooms under running water.
2. Slice the mushrooms very carefully lengthways, keeping the stalk and cap attached to each other for the centre slices.

3. Put a little fat into the frying pan over a moderate heat and allow it to get hot.
4. Put the mushrooms into the pan and fry them on both sides for about 5 minutes.

Baked onions *

What you need

1 large onion for each person
Salt and pepper
Butter or margarine
A little milk
Sharp knife
Ovenproof casserole or pie dish
Spoon

What to do

1. Trim the roots and tops off the onions and take off all the brown layers of skin.
2. Arrange the onions in the ovenproof dish.
3. Sprinkle with salt and pepper.
4. Put enough milk into the dish to come about a third of the way up the onions.
5. Put a small knob of butter on top of each onion.
6. Bake in a moderate oven (Electric 350 °F., Gas 4) for about 1 hour until tender right through.
7. While the onions are cooking spoon milk over them several times.
8. Serve in a hot serving dish with any liquid left in the baking dish.

Fried onions — for 4 people **

What you need

2 or 3 large onions
Dripping or cooking oil
Salt and pepper
Frying pan and fish-slice
Sharp knife and chopping board

What to do

1. Trim the roots and tops off the onions and take off all the brown layers of skin.
2. Cut the onions in half, place them cut side down and slice them into long strips.
3. Put the fat into the frying pan over a moderate heat and let it get hot.
4. Add onions, salt and pepper.
5. Fry the onions over a moderate heat until they are tender and deep golden brown. While they are cooking turn them occasionally to stop them burning.
6. Serve with grilled meat or sausages.

Peas — for 4 to 6 people ★★

What you need

2 pounds (900 grammes) peas
Salt
Sprig of mint
Butter or margarine
1 teaspoonful sugar
Saucepan
Colander or large strainer

What to do

1. Shell the peas and throw away any discoloured ones.
2. Quarter fill the pan with water and bring to the boil.
3. Add a pinch of salt and put the peas carefully into the boiling water.
4. Add the mint and a teaspoonful of sugar.
5. Simmer over a low heat until the peas are tender.
6. Drain the peas in the colander and return them to the pan.

7. Add a knob of butter and reheat gently until the butter is melted.
8. Put the peas into a hot serving dish and serve immediately.

Creamed spinach — for 4 people ★★★

What you need

2 pounds (900 grammes) spinach
1 ounce (30 grammes) butter or margarine
2 tablespoonfuls cream (this can be left out)
Salt and pepper
Large saucepan
Sharp knife
Colander
Wooden spoon

What to do

1. Wash the spinach very thoroughly under running water and remove any brown or damaged parts.
2. Break off the stalks and any coarse central ribs.
3. Put the wet leaves into the saucepan *without* any more water.
4. Put the pan over a low heat and cook slowly until the spinach is tender. Keep a lid on the pan but stir it occasionally.
5. Turn the spinach into the colander and press the water out with the back of the wooden spoon.
6. Put the butter into the pan over a moderate heat and allow it to melt.
7. Put the spinach back into the pan and reheat it.
8. Add the cream (if it is being used), salt and pepper and stir well.
9. Put into a hot serving dish and serve immediately.

Grilled tomatoes *

What you need

1 large tomato for each person
Salt and pepper
Butter or margarine
A little cheese (this can be left out)
Grill pan
Sharp knife
Cheese grater (if cheese is being used)

What to do

1. Wash the tomatoes and cut them in half along the equator.
2. Place the halves on the wire tray of the grill pan, cut side up.
3. Sprinkle them with salt and pepper.
4. Put a small knob of butter in the centre of each tomato half.
5. If cheese is being used, grate it and cover the top of each half tomato with grated cheese.
6. Turn on the grill and let it get hot.
7. Grill the tomatoes until the flesh is soft and the tops lightly browned.
8. Serve with grilled chops or at breakfast with bacon.

Mashed turnip or swede — for 4 people **

What you need

1 large turnip or swede
Butter or margarine
Salt and pepper
Large saucepan
Sharp knife and chopping board

Colander
Potato masher or large fork

What to do

1. Wash the turnip thoroughly and peel it thickly.
2. Cut the flesh into fairly square pieces.
3. Put the turnip into the saucepan with a pinch of salt and add just enough water to cover it.
4. Bring to the boil over a moderate heat with the lid on, turn down the heat and simmer until the turnip is tender. This may take an hour or more.
5. Drain the turnip in the colander and return it to the saucepan.
6. Add a large knob of butter, salt and pepper, and mash them all together thoroughly.
7. Reheat over a very low heat and turn into a hot serving dish. Serve immediately.

A few carrots can be added to the mashed turnip. Put sliced carrots into the same pan after the turnip has been cooking for about 40 minutes.

Boiled rice — for 4 people **

What you need

6 ounces (170 grammes) long grained rice
Salt
Saucepan
Wooden spoon
Fine-mesh strainer

What to do

1. Half fill the pan with water and bring to the boil over a moderate heat.
2. Put the rice into the strainer and wash it under running water.

3. Put the rice, and a pinch of salt, into the boiling water.
4. Keep the water boiling over a moderate heat until the rice is soft, stirring it occasionally to stop the grains sticking together. Add more water if it boils dry.
5. Drain the rice in the strainer and rinse it with fresh hot water.
6. Put it into a hot serving dish and leave it in a cool oven for 5 minutes (Electric 300 °F., Gas 2) to dry slightly before serving.

Chapter 12

HOW TO MAKE
SWEETS AND PUDDINGS

Fresh fruit and cream — for 4 people ★

What you need

½ pound (225 grammes) strawberries or raspberries
¼ pint (140 millilitres) single or double cream
A little sugar
4 fruit dishes
Mixing bowl and whisk or large fork (if double cream is used)
Small jug

What to do

1. Wash the fruit carefully under running water and remove any stalks.
2. Pile the fruit into fruit dishes and sprinkle with sugar.
3. If you are using single cream, serve it in a jug on the table.
4. If you are using double cream, put it into the mixing bowl.
5. Sprinkle in a teaspoonful of sugar.
6. Whip the double cream until it goes thick.
7. Either serve the whipped cream in a jug on the table with a spoon, or spoon it in heaps on top of the fruit in the dishes.

Fresh fruit salad *

What you need

1 apple
1 pear
1 banana
1 orange
A few grapes or cherries
¼ pint (140 millilitres) water
3 ounces (85 grammes) sugar
Lemon juice
1 tablespoonful brandy, sherry or maraschino (if you have
    any and if you like it)
Large fruit bowl
Small saucepan
Wooden spoon

What to do

1. Wash, peel and core the apple and pear and cut them
   into small pieces.
2. Peel the banana and cut into circles.
3. Wash the grapes or cherries and if possible take out the
   pips or stones.
4. Peel the orange, take out the pips and remove the white
   pith. Divide it into segments.
5. Put ¼ pint of water into the saucepan.
6. Add the sugar and bring to the boil over a moderate
   heat, stirring well. Then leave it to cool slightly.
7. Put all the fruit into the fruit bowl.
8. Add about a tablespoonful of lemon juice and the brandy
   (if it is being used) to the fruit and stir.
9. Spoon the warm syrup over the fruit and stir.

10. Leave the salad to cool, if possible in a refrigerator, before serving.
11. Serve with a jug of cream.

Fruit jelly ⋆

What you need

1 pint (560 millilitres) packet of fruit jelly cubes (raspberry flavour with a tin of raspberries, orange jelly with tinned oranges etc.)
1 small tin fruit
Mixing bowl
Jelly mould
Wooden spoon
Small saucepan with measurements on the side

What to do

1. Break the jelly into cubes and place in the mixing bowl.
2. Open the tin of fruit and drain the juice into the saucepan.
3. Make the liquid up to 1 pint with cold water.
4. Bring this mixture to the boil over a moderate heat.
5. Pour it on to the jelly cubes and stir until all the cubes have dissolved.
6. Put the fruit into the jelly and stir.
7. Rinse mould with cold water.
8. Pour the mixture into the jelly mould and leave in a cool place to set for several hours. (Do not put it in a refrigerator until it is cold.)
9. Turn the jelly into a dish or on to a plate to serve. If it is difficult to get out of the mould, warm the outside of the mould for a moment in hot water.
10. If the jelly will not set, dissolve another jelly cube or a teaspoonful of powdered gelatine in a very little boiling water and stir it into the mixture. Leave it to set again.

Junket *

What you need

1 pint (560 millilitres) milk
1 teaspoonful rennet
2 teaspoonfuls sugar
A little grated nutmeg
Small saucepan
Wooden spoon
Large glass dish

What to do

1. Warm the milk over a very low heat until it is just blood heat: test it by sipping a little from a teaspoon.
2. Stir in the sugar until it has dissolved.
3. Pour the milk into the glass dish.
4. Add the rennet and stir in well.
5. Leave the dish in a warm place until the junket has set. Cover the dish with a clean cloth or piece of paper to keep out the dust. If the junket fails to set add one more drop of rennet and leave to set again.
6. When it has set put it in a cool place, if possible in a refrigerator, to chill.
7. Just before serving, sprinkle a little grated nutmeg on top.
8. Serve with fruit.

Custard ** (to serve with hot puddings or to use in making cold sweets)

What you need

2 tablespoonfuls custard powder
2 tablespoonfuls sugar
1 pint (560 millilitres) milk

Small mixing bowl
Wooden spoon
Saucepan

What to do

1. Put the custard powder and sugar into the mixing bowl.
2. Add just enough milk to mix it to a smooth cream.
3. Put the rest of the milk into the saucepan and bring to the boil over a moderate heat.
4. Add the custard mixture to the hot milk, stirring all the time.
5. Bring the mixture back to the boil, stirring all the time.
6. Turn down the heat and simmer gently for 2 minutes.
7. If the custard is to be served with a pudding, serve in a warm jug. If it is needed especially thick for a cold sweet such as trifle it may help to add an extra ½ tablespoonful of custard powder to the mixture.

Banana custard ★★

What you need

1 pint (560 millilitres) custard (made according to the previous recipe)
2 or 3 bananas
Glacé cherries and angelica
Large glass dish
Sharp knife and chopping board

What to do

1. Make up the custard according to the previous recipe.
2. Leave the custard to cool slightly.
3. Peel the bananas and chop them into circles.
4. Put a layer of chopped banana on to the bottom of the dish.

5. Pour the cool custard on top of the banana.
6. Arrange the rest of the banana on top of the custard.
7. Leave to go cold in a cool place, if possible in a refrigerator (but do not put it into a refrigerator until it is almost cold).
8. Just before serving decorate the top with glacé cherries and angelica.

Trifle **

What you need

Sponge cake
Jam
Small tin of fruit
A little sherry (if available)
1 pint (560 millilitres) custard (made according to the recipe on page 124)
¼ pint (140 millilitres) double cream
Glacé cherries, angelica and/or chopped nuts
Large glass dish
Knife and spoon
Mixing bowl and whisk or large fork
Piping bag (if available)

What to do

1. Spread jam on the sponge cake and cut it into pieces so that it will cover the bottom of the glass dish.
2. Scatter the tinned fruit on top of the cake.
3. Add the juice from the fruit and the sherry (if it is used).
4. Leave to stand for about half an hour for the liquid to soak in.
5. While the trifle is standing, make the custard, and allow to cool.
6. Spoon the cooled custard on top of the fruit.

7. Put the cream into the mixing bowl and whisk it until it is stiff.
8. If you have a piping bag, fill it with cream and pipe it on to the top of the trifle in a pattern. If not, spoon the cream on to the trifle and decorate with a fork.
9. Decorate the top of the trifle with glacé cherries, angelica and/or chopped nuts.

Fruit fool ***

What you need

1 pound (450 grammes) gooseberries *or* blackcurrants *or* blackberries
2 tablespoonfuls sugar
1 tablespoonful water
¼ pint (280 millilitres) custard
½ pint (140 millilitres) double cream
Saucepan
1 large and 1 medium mixing bowl
Wooden spoon
Whisk or large fork
Sieve

What to do

1. Wash the fruit and remove the stalks.
2. Place them in the saucepan with the sugar and water.
3. Stew them gently until soft, and allow to cool.
4. Make the custard according to the recipe on page 124 and allow to cool.
5. Put the sieve over the large mixing bowl and rub the fruit into it with a wooden spoon; press hard on the spoon and rub it backwards and forwards.
6. Add the custard and mix well. Taste the mixture and add extra sugar if it is sour.

7. Whisk the cream in the other bowl until it begins to thicken.
8. Add the cream to the fruit mixture and stir in well.
9. Pour the fool into a large glass dish, or into individual dishes for each person.
10. Serve very cold with a piece of shortbread or a wafer for each person.

Rice pudding — for 4 people *

What you need

3 ounces (85 grammes) short-grained rice
1½ pints (840 millilitres) of milk
2 ounces (55 grammes) sugar
Butter
Grated nutmeg
Deep pie dish
Wooden spoon
Strainer

What to do

1. Grease the pie dish with butter.
2. Put the rice in the strainer and wash it under running water.
3. Put the rice in the pie dish.
4. Add the milk.
5. If possible, leave to stand for about half an hour.
6. Add the sugar and stir with a wooden spoon.
7. Sprinkle grated nutmeg on the surface.
8. Cut a good knob of butter into small pieces and scatter them on the surface.
9. Bake in a moderate oven (Electric 300 °F., Gas 2) for 2 hours until the pudding is brown on top and creamy underneath.
10. Serve it on its own, or with stewed fruit.

Semolina pudding — for 4 people ★★

What you need

2 ounces (55 grammes) semolina (or ground rice)
1½ pints (840 millilitres) of milk
2 ounces (55 grammes) sugar
Saucepan
Wooden spoon
Deep pie dish

What to do

1. Heat the milk in the saucepan over a moderate heat.
2. Sprinkle in the semolina, stirring all the time.
3. Boil the mixture until the semolina turns clear, stirring all the time.
4. Add the sugar and stir.
5. Pour the mixture into the pie dish.
6. Bake the pudding in a moderate oven (Electric 350 °F., Gas 4) for 20 to 30 minutes until brown on top.
7. Serve with jam or stewed fruit.

Bread and butter pudding — for 4 people ★★

What you need

4 slices of bread
Butter
Jam
½ pint (280 millilitres) of milk
1 egg
½ ounce (15 grammes) sugar
½ ounce (15 grammes) currants or sultanas
Grated nutmeg
Small saucepan

I

Mixing bowl
Whisk or large fork
Deep pie dish

What to do

1. Butter the slices of bread and spread them thinly with jam.
2. Heat the milk in the saucepan very slowly to about blood heat.
3. Whisk the egg and sugar together in the mixing bowl.
4. Add the warm milk and continue to whisk.
5. Put two slices of bread on the bottom of the pie dish jam side up.
6. Sprinkle the dried fruit on top of the bread.
7. Cover with the other two slices of bread, jam side down.
8. Pour the egg mixture over the bread.
9. Sprinkle a little grated nutmeg on top.
10. Leave the pudding to stand for about 30 minutes.
11. Bake in a moderate oven (Electric 350 °F., Gas 4) for 30 minutes.

Sponge pudding — for 4 people ★★

What you need

2 eggs
4 ounces (110 grammes) self-raising flour
4 ounces (110 grammes) margarine
4 ounces (110 grammes) sugar
1 tablespoonful milk
1 tablespoonful jam (or lemon curd, marmalade or syrup)
Mixing bowl and wooden spoon
Pudding mould or deep dish, or 4 small pudding moulds
Tablespoon

What to do

1. Grease the pudding mould and sprinkle flour inside to coat the surface.
2. Put the margarine and sugar into the mixing bowl and beat them together with a wooden spoon or fork until they turn pale in colour and look fluffy.
3. Add the eggs, one at a time, and beat in thoroughly.
4. Add the flour and mix in lightly.
5. Add the milk to make a runny mixture.
6. Put a good tablespoonful of jam into the bottom of the mould.
7. Pour the pudding mixture into the mould. Do not fill it more than two-thirds full.
8. Bake in a moderate oven (Electric 375 °F., Gas 5) for about 1 hour for a large pudding, about 20 minutes for 4 small puddings.
9. When it is done, turn the pudding on to a plate and pour any melted jam from the mould over the top.
10. Serve with a jug of hot custard, using the recipe on page 124.

Chocolate pudding — for 4 people ★★

What you need

4 ounces (110 grammes) self-raising flour
3 ounces (85 grammes) margarine
4 ounces (110 grammes) sugar
1 ounce (30 grammes) cocoa powder
2 eggs
Pinch of salt
2 tablespoonfuls milk
Few drops of vanilla essence
Mixing bowl and wooden spoon

Pudding basin or deep pie dish
Small mixing bowl
Whisk or large fork

What to do

1. Put the flour and a pinch of salt into the large mixing bowl.
2. Chop the margarine into small pieces and add to the flour.
3. Rub the fat into the flour with your fingers until it looks like fine bread crumbs.
4. Add the cocoa powder and mix well.
5. Whisk the eggs, sugar and milk in the small bowl.
6. Add the egg mixture to the flour and stir.
7. Add just enough milk to make a creamy mixture which drops off your spoon.
8. Add a few drops of vanilla essence and stir.
9. Pour into the greased pudding basin and bake in a fairly hot oven (Electric 375 °F., Gas 5) for 30 to 40 minutes until completely firm.
10. When it is done, turn the pudding onto a plate and sprinkle with sugar.
11. Serve with a jug of hot custard.

Baked jam roll — for 4 people ★★

What you need

8 ounces (225 grammes) self-raising flour
4 ounces (110 grammes) finely chopped suet or white cooking fat
Pinch of salt
Jam
Water
Mixing bowl and wooden spoon

Rolling pin and board
Knife
Flat baking tray

What to do

1. Mix the flour, salt and suet together in the mixing bowl.
2. Add the water slowly, mixing well, to make a soft dough.
3. Roll out the dough into an oblong about ¼ inch (6 millimetres) thick.
4. Spread jam over the dough, not quite to the edges.
5. Roll the dough up gently like a Swiss roll.
6. Seal the edges, using a little water to make them stick.
7. Put the roll on to the baking tray and bake in a hot oven
   (Electric 400 °F., Gas 6) for about 1 hour.
8. Put the roll on to a serving dish and serve with a jug of hot
   custard.

Baked apples *

What you need

1 cooking apple for each person
3 ounces (85 grammes) demerara sugar
Cup of water
2 ounces (55 grammes) dried fruit (currants, sultanas or
   raisins)
1 teaspoonful ground cinnamon
Small mixing bowl
Sharp knife
Ovenproof dish

What to do

1. Put the dried fruit, cinnamon and *half* the sugar into the
   mixing bowl and mix with a teaspoonful of water.
2. Wash the apples and take out the cores by cutting round

them carefully and pushing them out leaving a hollow centre to the fruit.
3. Put the apples in the dish.
4. Fill the centre of each apple with the fruit mixture.
5. Sprinkle the rest of the sugar over the apples.
6. Just cover the bottom of the dish with water.
7. Bake in a moderate oven (Electric 350 °F., Gas 4) for about 1 hour until the apples are soft right through.
8. Serve on their own or with a jug of hot custard.

Stewed fruit — for 4 people **★★**

What you need

1 pound (450 grammes) fruit (apples, rhubarb, gooseberries or blackcurrants)
2 to 4 ounces (55 to 110 grammes) sugar
2 tablespoonfuls water
Sharp knife
Medium saucepan with a close-fitting lid

What to do

1. Wash the fruit and prepare it; peel apples and slice the flesh; cut the leaves off rhubarb and cut into pieces; top and tail gooseberries or currants.
2. Put the prepared fruit into the saucepan with sugar and water.
3. Cover with the lid and put on a low heat.
4. Simmer until the fruit is soft, stirring occasionally to stop it sticking.
5. Taste and add more sugar if it is sour.
6. Serve in a glass dish with a jug of hot custard.

Eve's pudding — for 4 people **

What you need

1 pound (450 grammes) stewed apples (see the previous recipe)
4 ounces (110 grammes) butter or margarine
4 ounces (110 grammes) sugar
2 eggs
4 ounces (110 grammes) self-raising flour
Small lemon
Mixing bowl and wooden spoon
Deep pie dish
Grater

What to do

1. Stew the apples according to the previous recipe.
2. Grease the pie dish and put the apples on the bottom.
3. Put the butter and sugar into the mixing bowl and beat them together with a wooden spoon or fork until they turn pale in colour and look fluffy.
4. Add the eggs one at a time and beat in thoroughly.
5. Grate the rind from half the lemon and add the rind to the mixture.
6. Add the flour and mix in lightly.
7. Spread the mixture over the apples in the pie dish.
8. Bake in a moderate oven (Electric 350 °F., Gas 4) for about 40 minutes until the top is firm and golden brown.
9. Serve on its own or with a jug of hot custard.

Apple charlotte — for 4 people **

What you need

1½ pounds (670 grammes) cooking apples

3 ounces (85 grammes) brown sugar
1 lemon
6 slices of bread
Butter
Caster sugar
Deep pie dish
Grater
Greaseproof paper
Sharp knife

What to do

1. Grease the pie dish with butter, and butter the slices of bread.
2. Wash, peel and slice the apples.
3. Grate the rind off the lemon and cut it in half.
4. Place a layer of apple slices on the bottom of the pie dish.
5. Sprinkle with brown sugar, lemon rind and lemon juice from the lemon halves.
6. Cover with slices of bread and butter.
7. Repeat the layers until the dish is full, finishing off with a layer of bread, butter side up.
8. Cut a piece of greaseproof paper the size of the dish and cover the pudding with it.
9. Bake in a moderate oven (Electric 350 °F., Gas 4) for 50 minutes.
10. When it is done, turn it out of the dish on to a hot serving plate and sprinkle caster sugar over it.

Fruit crumble — for 4 people ★★

What you need

1½ pounds (670 grammes) stewed fruit (recipe on page 134)
3 ounces (85 grammes) butter or margarine
6 ounces (170 grammes) plain flour

3 ounces (85 grammes) sugar
Mixing bowl and wooden spoon
Deep pie dish

What to do

1. Grease the pie dish with butter.
2. Put the stewed fruit on the bottom.
3. Put the butter and flour into the mixing bowl and rub them together with your fingers until they look like fine bread crumbs.
4. Mix in the sugar.
5. Sprinkle this mixture over the fruit and press down lightly.
6. Bake in a moderate oven (Electric 350 °F., Gas 4) until the top is golden brown.
7. When it is done, sprinkle sugar on the top and serve with a jug of hot custard.

Chapter 13

ALL ABOUT SALADS
AND SOME COLD DISHES

Salads often look or taste boring just because they are made with the same ingredients time after time: lettuce, tomato and cucumber. In fact a salad can make an interesting meal if you take the trouble to vary what goes into it. So here are some suggestions for salad ingredients, and how to prepare them, which can be used in different combinations all the year round.

A salad is also made much more tasty by adding a suitable dressing. There are three recipes for salad dressings for you to try for yourselves, although of course you can also use the bottled salad dressings available from the shops.

Some people feel that mayonnaise is difficult to make at home. It is true that it can go wrong, and curdle, that is, turn lumpy rather like scrambled egg. But like most things, it can be rescued when things go wrong so do not worry too much. In any case, if you follow the instructions carefully you should have no trouble making a mayonnaise that your family will really appreciate.

What to choose

Naturally you must choose vegetables which are available at home or which you can buy in the shops. Some are available only at certain seasons of the year. But in general, try to choose one vegetable that is green, one which is brightly coloured, and one which is crisp or hard. Three or four are usually enough for a good mixed salad.

In winter too

You can still make tasty salads in winter even though there may be no lettuces or tomatoes in the shops. Experiment with winter vegetables such as cabbage, carrots and cauliflower eaten raw.

Lettuce, chicory and endive ★

All these vegetables can form the basis of a mixed salad or be served on their own with a French dressing, so do not always rely on lettuce. They all make a good green salad to serve instead of a hot vegetable with a hot meat dish, served on a small side-plate or bowl.

What to do

1. Cut across the thick stalk at the base of the vegetable.
2. Wash one leaf at a time under running water.
3. Shake the leaves in a colander or salad shaker to remove the water.
4. If possible, put the leaves in a closed salad box in the refrigerator for about 30 minutes to crisp them.
5. Break the leaves into pieces and serve in a glass or wooden bowl with dressing, or in a mixed salad.

Tomatoes ★

Tomatoes can either be used in a mixed salad or on their own with a little chopped onion or spring onion and a French dressing.

What to do

1. Wash the tomatoes.

2. Fill a basin with boiling water and put the tomatoes into the water so that they are completely covered.
3. After 1 minute, take the tomatoes out and you will find that the skin will peel off easily.
4. Slice the skinned tomatoes and put into a serving bowl.

Apples *

Apples make an interesting addition to a mixed salad and go especially well with cucumber.

What to do

1. Wash, peel and core 2 or 3 eating apples.
2. Slice the flesh thinly and mix with sliced cucumber and lemon juice, or chop into cubes and add to a mixed salad.

Beetroot *

Beetroot can either be served on its own or in a mixed salad.

What to do

1. Boil raw beetroot until tender and allow to cool in its own juice.
2. Drain them and peel them carefully.
3. Cut into slices and put into a serving dish with vinegar and a little water, or chop into cubes and add to a mixed salad.

Cabbage *

In winter raw cabbage can be used as the green vegetable in a mixed salad, and it makes an interesting addition at any time.

What to do

1. Cut off the main coarse stalk and throw away any discoloured leaves.

2. Wash the cabbage leaf by leaf under running water.
3. Shred the cabbage finely with a sharp knife and add to mixed salad.

Carrots *

Carrots make a colourful addition to mixed salad. They go well with raw cabbage and beetroot.

What to do

1. Scrub the carrots and peel them if the skin is very thick.
2. Either grate the carrots finely and add to a mixed salad, or grate them and serve separately with a few sultanas and sprinkled with lemon juice.

Cauliflower *

Cauliflower can also be eaten raw and makes an attractive addition to a mixed salad. Cold cooked cauliflower is also good sprinkled with lemon juice and parsley.

What to do

1. Wash the cauliflower thoroughly and cut off the thick stalks and the leaves.
2. Break the flower into small sprigs and add to mixed salad.

Celery *

Raw celery can either be served on its own in sticks or chopped and added to a mixed salad. It goes especially well with cheese.

What to do

1. Chop the hard root section off the head of celery and remove any discoloured leaves from the top.

2. Separate the sticks and scrub them under running water.
3. Either serve the celery whole in a tall celery dish, or chop the sticks across into small pieces and add to a mixed salad.

Cucumber **

Cucumber is sometimes served alone and is a popular addition to a summer mixed salad. It goes especially well with sliced apple.

What to do

1. Wash the cucumber and slice it as thinly as possible.
2. Sprinkle it with salt and leave for 30 minutes.
3. Drain off the water.
4. Put it in a serving dish with a little vinegar or lemon juice or add it to a mixed salad.

Eggs *

Hard-boiled eggs are often added to a mixed salad and go especially well with a mayonnaise dressing.

What to do

1. Hard boil the eggs (follow the recipe on page 93).
2. Put them under cold running water to cool them.
3. Shell the eggs carefully and slice them across and add to a mixed salad.

Mustard and cress and water cress *

These are popular additions to mixed salads. Mustard and cress goes well with hard-boiled eggs, and water cress with cold meats.

What to do

1. Wash the cress very thoroughly under running water.
2. Shake the leaves in a colander or salad shaker to remove the water. Add to a mixed salad.

Onions and spring onions **

Spring onions can be served on their own or as part of a mixed salad, and large chopped onions make a tasty addition to a mixed salad. Onions go especially well with cheese, and mixed with tomatoes and green or red peppers.

What to do

1. Cut off the roots and tops of large onions and take off the brown layers of skin. Cut off the roots and any discoloured leaves of spring onions and take off the outer layer of skin if it is discoloured.
2. Wash thoroughly.
3. Chop large onions into small pieces or strips. Either serve spring onions whole or chop across into small circles. Add either kind of chopped onion to a mixed or a tomato salad.

Peas and beans *

Cold, cooked peas and beans can be added to a mixed salad and this is a useful way of using them up if they are left over from an earlier meal.

What to do

1. Simply add cooked peas or broad beans to a mixed salad.
2. Chop cooked French beans and add to mixed salad with French dressing.

Peppers **

Red and green peppers, available at certain times of the year, make a colourful addition to a mixed salad. They go especially well with onions and tomatoes.

What to do

1. Wash the pepper and cut out the stalk with a sharp knife.
2. Slit the pepper in two and remove all the seeds and pith.
3. Cut the halves of pepper into long strips and add to mixed salad.

Pineapple **

Pineapple, either tinned or fresh, makes an interesting addition to a mixed salad and goes especially well with cheese and ham.

What to do

1. Cut fresh pineapple across into thick slices and then cut the flesh into cubes.
2. Add fresh or tinned cubes to mixed salad.

Potatoes **

Potatoes are usually made into a special salad and served separately from other salad vegetables. Here is a recipe for a simple potato salad.

What you need — for 4 people

3 large new potatoes
1 small onion or 3 spring onions
Parsley
Mint

Salt and pepper
2 teaspoonfuls single cream
1 tablespoonful olive oil
1 teaspoonful vinegar
Saucepan
Sharp knife and chopping board
Small mixing bowl and wooden spoon

What to do

1. Wash and peel the potatoes and boil them until they are tender. Leave to cool.
2. Chop the onion and a sprig of parsley and mint as finely as possible.
3. Put the cream and salt and pepper into the mixing bowl.
4. Add the oil drop by drop, stirring well all the time.
5. Add the vinegar drop by drop, still stirring.
6. Chop the cold potatoes into cubes and put in a serving dish.
7. Sprinkle with chopped onion, parsley and mint.
8. Pour over the cream dressing and if possible serve chilled.

Melon **

Melon can be served either as a cold first course or as a sweet.

What to do

1. Slice the melon into 6 or 8 segments.
2. Very carefully cut between the flesh and the skin of each segment, leaving the flesh in place.
3. Now cut downwards from the top of the

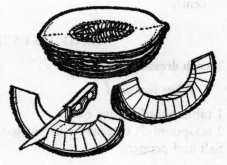

K

flesh to the skin, so that the flesh is now in small pieces which can easily be lifted off.

4. Serve in individual dishes and place bowls of sugar and ground ginger on the table. Provide either a small knife and fork or a spoon and fork with which to eat the melon.

Grapefruit **

Grapefruit is often served at breakfast or as a first course at dinner.

What to do

1. Cut the grapefruit in half with a sharp knife round the 'equator'.
2. Cut carefully along the edge of the skin to loosen the flesh, cutting right through the pithy parts which divide the flesh into segments.
3. Loosen each segment but leave them in place.
4. Sprinkle a little sugar on top of the grapefruit halves and serve in fruit dishes. For dinner the halves can be decorated with a glacé cherry in the centre.

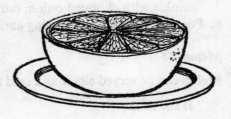

SALAD DRESSINGS

French dressing *

What you need

1 tablespoonful olive oil
2 teaspoonfuls vinegar (wine vinegar if you can get it)
Salt and pepper

Sugar
Mustard (if liked)
Chopped herbs (if liked)
Mixing bowl and wooden spoon *or* a bottle with a screw top.

What to do

1. *Either* put the oil, vinegar, a pinch of salt and pepper, ½ a
   teaspoonful of sugar into the mixing bowl and mix them
   thoroughly until the dressing goes thick *or* put the same
   ingredients into the bottle, screw the top on tightly and
   shake it until the dressing goes thick.
2. Add either a teaspoonful of made mustard or some
   chopped herbs if you like either of these.

Cream salad dressing ★★

What you need

2 teaspoonfuls single cream
1 tablespoonful olive oil
1 teaspoonful vinegar
Salt and pepper
Mustard (if liked)
Mixing bowl and wooden spoon

What to do

1. Mix together a mustardspoonful of made mustard, the
   cream and a pinch of salt and pepper.
2. Add the oil drop by drop, stirring well all the time.
3. Add the vinegar drop by drop, still stirring.

Mayonnaise ★★★

What you need

1 egg yolk
Salt and pepper

Mustard (if liked)
Olive oil
Vinegar or lemon juice
Mixing bowl and wooden spoon

What to do

1. Separate the egg yolk from the white. Do this by breaking the egg in half very carefully over a cup. Let the yolk stay in one half of the shell and let the white run out into the cup. Then put the yolk into your mixing bowl.
2. Add a pinch of salt and pepper and a mustardspoonful of made mustard and beat them together well.
3. Add a few drops of vinegar or lemon juice and beat well.
4. Add olive oil, a drop at a time, stirring well all the time.
5. When the mixture is so thick that the spoon will stand up in it, thin it down by adding more vinegar a drop at a time and stirring.
6. Then add more oil, drop by drop, stirring well. Continue to add vinegar and oil alternately in this way until you have enough mayonnaise.
7. If the mixture curdles, that is, goes rather like soft scrambled eggs, put another egg yolk into a clean basin and mix the curdled mixture into it a drop at a time, beating it thoroughly. Then start adding vinegar and oil again. The finished mayonnaise should be smooth and creamy.

Chapter 14

HOW TO PLAN A MENU

Cooking a whole meal for your family is more difficult than cooking just one dish, so plan what you are going to make carefully in advance. And remember the basic rule, collect together *everything* you will need before you start any preparations. This will mean checking the list at the top of *every* recipe.

What to make?

The first decision to make is what to have as the main dish. This may depend on what is in the house, or you may be able to do your own shopping—but decide on the fish, meat, egg or cheese course first and then think of the rest of the meal as an accompaniment to the main course. Make your decisions like this:

1. What main dish shall I have?
2. How will it be cooked?
3. What vegetables does it need with it?
4. What sort of second course shall I have?

What main dish shall I have? And how to cook it?

Even if your main item is provided for you by your mother, you can at least decide on the way it should be cooked. So choose a recipe and when you know whether it will be cooked on top of the cooker or in the oven, see if you can cook some other parts of the meal the same way.

What vegetables does it need?

The choice of vegetables depends on several factors. Does the main dish have any vegetables cooked with it? If so you will not need many others. One may be enough.

Not all vegetables are available all the year round so this will limit your choice. It is no good hoping to cook fresh garden peas in England in December.

Does your family dislike any particular vegetable? If so try to find one which everybody enjoys.

What is the weather like? This may seem an odd question but no one wants to eat a heavy stew and two vegetables on a hot summer day or a completely cold meal on a frosty day. So stick to winter days for hot and very filling meals and experiment with salads in warmer weather.

Finally decide whether you can cook your vegetables the same way as the meat.

What sort of second course?

The second course should fit in with the first: in winter a cold sweet can follow a hot dinner and in summer a cold pudding and a cold main course is quite acceptable.

Should it be a heavy baked pudding or something lighter? Again this depends on the main course: in winter your family may enjoy a filling dinner and a filling sweet, but usually it is best to have one course light and one course heavy. Do not make your meals too stodgy or your family will get fat.

Finally decide if you can cook your pudding in the same way as the meat or the vegetables.

This is especially important if you are cooking in the oven: the oven has more than one shelf and can easily be used to cook two or three parts of the meal. So remember that vegetables can be braised as well as boiled and that some puddings can be baked. Alternatively if you are cooking the main dish on the top of the cooker try to find recipes for the vegetables and pudding which can also be done on top. It is seldom worth switching on the oven just for one dish.

Do what you can in advance

Make some dishes in advance if you can—cold sweets and baked tarts and cakes can even be done the day before. Salads too can be prepared in advance but do not put the dressing on until the last minute.

How long will it take?

A meal will take a little longer to prepare than the slowest dish on the menu. So look at your chosen recipes and find out which dish will take the longest to cook: most often this will be the meat, which cooks slowly, or it may be a pudding which has to be baked or which will set slowly.

Add time for preparation to the cooking time of each recipe and then make a plan of the jobs you have to do:

$1\frac{1}{2}$ hours

MEAT ————————————————————————→

1 hour

PUDDING ————————————————————→

$\frac{1}{2}$ hour

VEGETABLES ——————————→

11-30   12-0   1-0
                                              Dinner time

From this sort of plan it is quite clear which job has to be done first if all the food is going to be ready at the right time. So do the jobs in the right order and you will not spoil the

food by keeping some dishes waiting to be served because
something else is not done in time. You can make this sort of
plan for any meal, however many jobs there are to be done.
Just add another time line for each job to be done.

SUGGESTED MENUS

Here are some suggested menus chosen from recipes in this
book:

Breakfast

Grapefruit halves
Grilled sausages and tomatoes

Fruit juice
Poached eggs on toast

Lunch or dinner

Minced beef with onions
Mashed potatoes
Buttered carrots
Stewed fruit and junket

Spaghetti bolognese
Gooseberry fool

Grilled chicken with sweetcorn
Grilled tomatoes
New potatoes
Fruit jelly with cream

Irish stew
Buttered cabbage
Fruit crumble

Braised beef
Baked potatoes
Braised celery or leeks
Baked apples and custard

Cold meat
Salad of tomatoes, onions, peppers and cucumber
Baked jam roll and custard (on a cool day)
or Banana custard (on a warm day)

Now you should be able to choose your own recipes. Good
luck.

INDEX

155